I0069037

This book is a Water Training Institute *Travel Companion* and is designed to be read in its entirety during a round-trip airline flight

The ART of MOVEMENT

ALSO BY TAB EDWARDS

THE WATER TRAINING INSTITUTE · SINCE 1987

TAB EDWARDS

The
Art *of*
MOVEMENT

*The Philosophy of Professional Selling
and Why Some Sellers are More Effective
than Others Over the Long Term*

T

TMBE, PHILADELPHIA, PENNSYLVANIA 19129

TMBE / *The Water Training Institute*

ISBN 978-0-9700891-4-4

This publication is designed to provide authoritative information in regards to the subject matter covered. It is sold with the understanding that the publisher is not engaged in rendering legal, accounting, or other professional services. If legal advice or other expert assistance is required, the services of a competent professional person should be sought.

—From a declaration of principles jointly adopted by a committee of the American Bar Association and a committee of publishers.

Tab Edwards books are available at special quantity discounts to use as premiums and promotions, or for use in corporate training programs. For more information, please visit the website TabEdwards.com.

Designed by Water Creative
Philadelphia, PA.

1   3   5   7   9   10   8   6   4   2

TTX

C

Table *of* Contents

The
ART
of
MOVEMENT

i

What is "Selling"?

What exactly is "selling"? According to *Webster's Dictionary*, selling is the exchange of a product or service for money; to offer something for sale. Technically, this definition is fundamentally correct. However, I have a different view of what it means to "sell." I believe that selling is the art of extracting and clearly defining those things which challenge a person's comfortable existence, and gaining his or her confidence that you have access to "something" that will alleviate the discomfort, while persuading the person to believe that what you have is better for the person than anything anyone else can provide; It is the art of convincing a person to believe as you want them to believe, and to behave as you want them to behave. Selling is ***The Art of Movement***. It is the art of taking a person from some initial, disinclined position or mindset and "moving" them to a position where they share your vision and accept your recommendation because they believe it to be in their best interest.

Conditions Required to Really "Sell"

Based on my experience as a salesman selling in various situations to companies of various types, sizes, complexities and markets, combined with my experience as a sales trainer, researcher, and buyer-advocate, I believe a person only really *sells* when at least three conditions exist:

1. There must be an element of persuasion involved; you must convince someone to see your point of view

There is a saying that "people can't smell themselves." The meaning behind this saying is that, because people are *around* themselves every waking moment and are constantly living with their bodily scent, they become desensitized to their own smell unless they just ran a marathon, wrestled with pigs, or engaged in some other activity that makes their malodorous bodily aromas obvious. It often takes a friend or family member to tell the foul-smelling person, "You stink!" before the person realizes the need to take a shower.

As a seller, you must tell prospective buyers *they stink* (a metaphor for the fact that they have a problem they must address). You must convince prospective buyers to acknowledge your findings (that they smell bad) and move them to realize they *need* your proposition even when they don't fully realize they need it or when they initially tell you they don't want it. In this regard, the old axiom is correct: "Selling doesn't begin until the customer says 'NO'."

2. **Formidable competitive offerings must exist and must be known and available to the prospective buyer**

If you are the only game in town, then a prospective buyer has no choice except to buy your offering. This is not selling because, based on my definition of selling, you don't have to convince the prospect that your offering is better for them than anything anyone else can provide. If a prospective buyer has viable options available to him or her to purchase, you are then required to engage in the art of persuasion, the art or convincing, *The Art of Movement.* For instance, if you live in a small town with only one general store and that store only sells Nike sneakers, you, as the Nike salesperson at the store, don't have to convince the sneaker-buying customer to purchase the Nike brand—they have no choice; no selling required. If, on the other hand, there was a store across the road that sold Adidas sneakers and the prospective buyer was undecided between the two sneaker options, the Nike seller would have some work to do.

3. **The prospective buyer must be reluctant to meet with you because they don't want to have "some unscrupulous salesperson bugging them about spending money."**

Fact: No one likes dealing with salespeople. And because of this reluctance, most prospective buyers are defensive and closed-minded when first being approached by a seller. A big part of the sales process is convincing a prospective buyer to give you the opportunity to tell your story. If the situation exists where the prospect is reluctant to meet with you, your salespersonship comes into play as you try to convince the prospective buyer why it would be of value to him or her to meet with you. On the other hand, if a prospective buyer proactively solicits a meeting with you, they are either interested in the prospect of buying what you have to sell or, at a minimum, interested in being convinced to buy what you have to sell. In this situation, very little selling (if any) would be involved, and your role will be more information-provider and order-taker, than *seller*.

Nowadays, regardless of their job titles, most salespeople are order-takers, customer service representatives, account servicers, and account *managers*. The requirement for salespeople to actually *sell* has diminished over the years and, as a result, most salespeople either don't really know how to sell or their skills are diminishing instead of improving. Selling is like any other skill: if you don't practice it and continually learn the craft in order to improve, it's inevitable you will be worse a year from now than you are today.

Why has the requirement to actually *sell* diminished? The reasons are several-fold. One reason is the advancements in technology, giving buyers access to information, easy ordering platforms, and global sources of products, goods, and services that were unavailable to them just a short time ago. Another reason is because of the complexity of many products and services today. In many cases, products today are so complex (such as financial instruments, computer systems, and technology-related products), that buyers now have greater knowledge of the products and the value that can be extracted from them than does the salesperson. And when the buyer has greater knowledge than the person selling the product, equal access to information about the product, and global alternate sources for the product, the seller becomes nothing more than a facilitator for the knowledgeable buyer.

Consider this example. You are an automobile designer who, as a hobby, builds cars from scratch. You go into your local auto dealership to look at cars for possible purchase. As you enter the dealership, some rookie salesman approaches you and tries to "sell" you a car. In this example, there is nothing the car salesman can tell you—the expert—about a car, other than the non-public terms & conditions at that dealership. Therefore, in this scenario, the salesperson has little value to you and becomes nothing more than a person who facilitates your purchase. In this example, the salesman doesn't have to really *sell*; he is simply an order-taker. And to make matters worse for this salesperson, the prospective car buyer can test drive the car, kick the tires, and then go to one of the many on-line car buyer websites to purchase the same car, leaving the salesperson without a sale and without a commission. This is one of the realities about selling today: advances in technology have made it easier for buyers to execute purchase transactions without the services of a salesperson.

Much of selling has to do with the buyer's comfort level with the seller; it has to do with qualified opportunities; it has to do with the environmental conditions surrounding the prospective buyer; it has to do with the information and access available to the buyer; it has to do with the support infrastructure available to the seller; it has to do with luck; it has to do with competitors; and it has to do with more than simply following a step-by-step selling methodology. Today, the best sellers benefit from their experiences, their ability to understand he psyche of the buyer, their guile at moving prospective buyers from closed-mindedness and skepticism to open-mindedness and interest. The best sellers today have a knack for making *themselves* (as representatives of their companies) valuable to prospective buyers so that, when *real* sales opportunities do exist, they capitalize on them.

So, given my definition of what it is to *sell*, who actually sells anymore? Before they "died," encyclopedia salespeople (one of my past sales jobs) were the purest of salespeople: No one wanted to speak to them; they sold a product that no one really *needed*; they sold door-to-door and they mostly went on unsolicited cold-calls; they had to convince and persuade people that they *needed* the encyclopedias, not simply *wanted* them; and theirs was a product that people usually purchased with their disposable income, meaning the encyclopedia salesperson had to compete with family vacations, new shoes, groceries, and everything else for the prospective buyers' disposal income.

While door-to-door encyclopedia salespeople are a thing of the past, there are sellers across all industries who still *do* actually sell and who bring to mind the days of the encyclopedia sellers' impressive abilities to open doors, get invited into the living rooms, get the prospective buyers to lower their guard against sales-people, and move the buyers to a sale.

01

Customer Buying Emotions

Psychologists and sales thinkers alike agree that buyers make purchase decisions on two levels: *logical* and *emotional.* Logical decisions are made based on such things as product specifications (specs), performance ratings, price, and other tangible criteria of the sort. Emotional motivations include things that give us a sense of comfort, security, achievement, and other personal feelings of a job well done. It is often said that professionals should remove emotion from making business decisions and should make such decisions based on logic. The problem with introducing emotion into a business decision, it is argued, is that the decision-maker runs the risk of making a decision that is not in the best business interest of his or her company. Such "poor" business decisions can negatively impact a company's performance as well as its associates. In light of this business best-practice of making decisions based on logic, it is surprising to many that buyers primarily make purchase decisions based on *emotion* not *logic*. The *emotional* reasons often include:

- *Job Security*: the purchase decision will help the decision-maker keep his or her job and progress within the company, including financially.

- *Convenience*: to the decision-maker, the decision is the comfortable, easy decision to make.

- *Peace of Mind*: the decision-maker has confidence in the decision that it is a safe choice.

- *Recognition*: the decision-maker believes the purchase decision will earn kudos and props.

These decision processes are all based on emotion—how the purchase decision will affect the buyer personally. Remember that old saying that "No one has ever gotten fired for buying IBM"? One reason is because, many years ago, it was hard to argue with the choice of buying an IBM mainframe computer, for instance, because purchasers knew that they would be supported tremendously by IBM if a problem occurred, and IBM would "make the situation right." The purchase of an IBM mainframe computer provided convenience and peace of mind—*emotional* motivations.

Since, as I have established above, emotion does factor into buyers' purchase decisions, sellers have to account for this reality as they engage with prospective buyers, specifically, how emotional purchase decisions can slow, derail, or end a sales engagement. When it comes to the impact a buyer's emotions can have on a purchase decision or a sale, I refer to such impactful emotions as "Customer Buying Emotions."

I believe there are five primary impactful customer buying emotions that require and/or involve buyer-*movement*:

1. Fear
2. Skepticism
3. Calm & Openness
4. Interest
5. Action Mode

The *Customer Buying Emotions* describe the feelings that act as motivational energies leading prospective buyers to act in different ways when engaged in the process of the purchase (sale), actions ranging from stopping the buying (selling) process to signing a contract to make a purchase. Although these five sentiments may not technically be classified as "emotions"—research published in Current Biology says the range of *emotions* is only between four and six: happy, sad, afraid/surprised, and angry/disgusted—I use the sentiments here to refer to thoughts *influenced by or proceeding from emotion.* So, for the purposes of this book, I will refer to these sentiments of fear, skepticism, calm & openness, interest, and action mode as Buying *Emotions.*

Customer Buying Emotions can be viewed as stages that a prospective buyer goes through that begin with apprehension (fear and skepticism)—thus requiring movement on the part of the seller—and end with the customer fully engaged and poised to make a purchase decision (action mode). Each stage or Buying Emotion is sequential, and presents the seller with a different degree of difficulty in closing a sale. The beginning stages or initial Buying Emotions of *fear* and *skepticism* present the greatest barriers to moving the sale forward because, until a prospective buyer's fears are allayed and skepticism put to rest, the buyer will perceive that a purchase is risky (negatively impacting the decision-maker and the company) and the seller WILL NOT be able to move the process forward. This will lead to an elongated sales cycle, at best, and a stalled sales opportunity at worst. Once the buyer's fears are allayed he is no longer afraid of making the purchase decision but he does, however, remain skeptical of the seller's proposition. And when the buyer's skepticism is alleviated, the buyer's emotion then shifts to calm and openness, wherein the buyer's reluctance to act due to the perceived risk of a purchase is replaced by a measure of comfort, believing that the seller is willing to work with the buyer to help the buyer make a good business decision. This level of comfort also leads the buyer to become open to suggestions made by the seller, a willingness to consider doing things differently, and a genuine interest in the options available to the buyer for achieving his or her business objectives. Finally, after the buyer has developed an interest in the seller's proposition and a belief that the proposition will help the buyer do his job more effectively, the buyer will move into action mode where the buyer is ready to make a decision and execute a purchase transaction.

CUSTOMER BUYING EMOTIONS
And the Associated Length of the Sales / Buying Cycle

Shorten the Sales Cycle and improve your odds of gaining the sale by reducing the Customer Buying Emotions of Fear, Skepticism, and the lack of interest, thus Moving the deal process forward

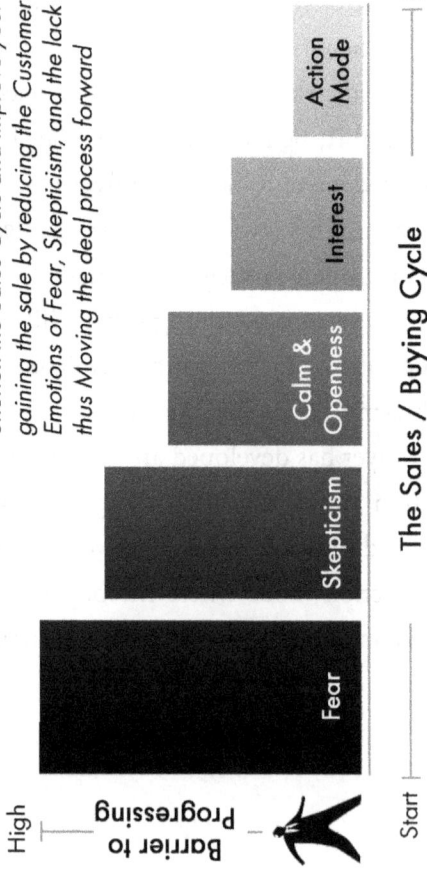

Fear	Skepticism	Calm & Openness	Interest	Action Mode

High — Barrier to Progressing

Start ———————— The Sales / Buying Cycle ———————— Purchase

The Customer Buying-Emotions Defined

The "Fear" Buying Emotion

Emotions—unlike physiological needs such as hunger—are typically brought on by cognition and reasoning in human beings as opposed to an intrinsic need. When we fear something, for instance, we do so because we think of the threat of harm brought on by the thing of which we think. If we are walking alone in the woods and we think that we might encounter a bear, we become fearful of the possibility. If we are sitting in our business office, however, the thought of a bear would not induce fear for two reasons: (1) It is unlikely that a bear would make its way into our office (reasoning), so the threat of harm brought on by a bear is minuscule; and (2) chances are that we would not even be *thinking* about a bear (cognition) in the first place. What we do think about when sitting in our office, however, is the threat of harm that would be brought on by making a bad, costly, or negatively-impactful business decision. This introduces the notion if *risk*.

Risk is the exposure to or consequences of making a costly decision, with *costly* being defined as having a negative, harmful, undesired impact. Business professionals make lots of business decisions in the course of a day, and they go to great lengths to understand, forestall, and mitigate any risk associated with those decisions. If a decision is determined to be *risky*, the potential for a negative outcome of that decision will induce *fear* in the decision maker based on the seriousness of the potential negative impact of that decision on the decision maker's business; this is the case with many purchase decisions that customers make. One of the primary contributors to a decision's riskiness is the amount of uncertainty inherent in a decision. If, for instance, the customer is making a decision to purchase a new, expensive piece of machinery with which the customer has no experience, the uncertainty of the machine's performance would make the purchase a somewhat risky one. And since we fear things in proportion to our lack of understanding of them, if the uncertainty of the machine's performance is high, the customer's perceived riskiness of the purchase decision will be high likewise; and the greater the perceived risk, the greater the customer's fear of making the purchase.

Risk Impact is the impact or effect the results of a decision will have on the buyer's company or the buyer personally should any of the risks associated with a purchase decision come to fruition. Buyers consider the potential risk impact—whether consciously or subconsciously—when making all significant purchase decisions. The perceived or actual potential negative outcome of a decision is directly correlated with a buyer's fear and trepidation of making that decision.

A buyer's uncertainty about aspects of a purchase alternative are primarily influenced by the buyer's knowledge of the performance of the product, service, or solution (based on experience); the level of credibility the buyer ascribes to the seller of the product, service, or solution; and the impact and magnitude of the of the damaged that would be caused if the buyer made a "bad" purchase (*risk impact*). For the buyer, the potential for a negative outcome is the risk that he or she assigns to a purchase decision. These three impacts on the *fear* emotion are presented below.

- *Knowledge/Experience*: A buyer's knowledge and familiarity with a product, service, or solution being considered for purchase are determined by experience with the item being considered. The experience can be direct—where the buyer has personally experienced the performance of the item being considered—or indirect, where the buyer is benefitting from the experience of someone else whom has had an experience with the item being considered. This is why many buyers request references from sellers that testify to the goodness and success of a product, service, or solution being considered by the buyer. These experiences contribute to the buyer's degree of *certainty* of the outcome of a purchase decision, and thus reduce the riskiness of a decision and the buyer's degree of fear associated with making a purchase.

- *Seller Credibility*: I believe that a seller's credibility is the most important characteristic a seller can possess. A seller's credibility not only applies to the seller's degree of trustworthiness and believability in the mind of the buyer, but it also extends to the seller's company and its products, services, and solutions, including their reliability, stability, and desirability as a company to do business with.

Credibility instills trust and confidence, which help assuage the *fear* and *skepticism* Buying Emotions, leading to calm and a shorter sales cycle. A "credible" seller is considered expert (experienced, qualified, intelligent and skilled) and trustworthy (honest, fair and caring), and being a credible resource to a buyer can facilitate a faster, more comfortable purchase decision by the buyer.

There are generally considered to be four types of credibility: presumed, reputed, surface and experienced.

Presumed credibility describes how we ascribe credibility to someone based on assumptions we make about that person. For example, most people assume their church pastor or priest tells the truth, so they view them as credible sources of information. On the contrary, people assume used-car salespeople are untruthful and, therefore, lack credibility and trustworthiness. The negative view of used-car salespeople is a stereotype, but that's the essence of presumed credibility: assumptions and stereotypes contribute to credibility perceptions.

Reputed credibility describes how we assign credibility to a person based on that person's reputation and what other people say about that person.

Surface credibility describes how we ascribe credibility to a person based on what we initially observe about that person. And as superficial and backward as it may sound, a person's "looks" and appearance can have an impact on the level of credibility a buyer ascribes to a seller. The way people dress or the language they use influences our perception of their credibility. That's why I believe a sales rep's degree of neatness and articulation are important qualities when interfacing with customers and prospective buyers.

Experienced credibility describes how we attribute credibility to someone based on first-hand experience. When we can witness—first hand—the job a person does for us, we are able to form our own opinions of how competent and trustworthy that person is. Presumed and Experienced credibility help most with alleviating buyers' *fear* and *skepticism* Buying Emotions.

Considerations for helping prospective buyers allay the fear of a purchase decision

Most buyers are tasked with a making an impactful decision that contains many uncertainties, including the uncertainty of the outcome of the purchase decision in many cases. This uncertainty and the potential exposure that comes with it make the decision a risky one for the buyer. Dealing with what the buyer considers to be "used-car salesmen/women" increases the buyer's perceived riskiness of the purchase because the buyer believes that the sellers only have their own interests in mind. This perception—whether real or imagined—puts buyers on alert for such "unscrupulous" sellers who they believe will go to any lengths to make a sale, even lying and deceit. This mindset puts the buyer on the defensive and makes it very difficult for the seller to convince the buyer to lower her guard and consider the benefits of the buyer's proposal.

When faced with such a situation, the sellers who are most successful at helping prospective buyers overcome the *fear* Buying Emotion and convincing them to lower their guard are those who:

1. *Establish credibility.* Some sellers come into a sales situation with reputed credibility based on their reputation. Others, however, often must earn the perception of credibility from the buyer's perspective. So, how does one earn credibility? Some best-practices for establishing credibility include:

   - Being responsible and reliable. Deliver what you promise and take responsibility for your actions. The easiest and quickest way to damage your credibility? Demonstrate irresponsibility and don't deliver what you promise.

   - Sharing your relevant experiences and highlighting your qualifications. Make the buyer aware of your relevant experiences and credentials in order to give them the confidence that doing business with you is not risky.

   - Being honest, even when it's painful to do so. Customers and prospective buyers know when you're being deceitful and, in the long-run, not being forthright and brutally honest—especially when the news is not good—can damage a seller's credibility as well.

- Demonstrating that you have the buyer's best interest at heart and that you both are interested in the success of the buyer's business-related endeavor; this is *consultative selling*, and research shows that those who sell consultatively establish higher levels of credibility and trust with buyers than those who do not.

- Being confident & assertive. Sellers should not be afraid to educate buyers or tell them they are wrong. Nothing says *uncredible* like a subordinate, uncertain, timid salesperson.

- Leveraging the credibility of other people. Highlight the credibility of your sources of information. Get an introduction or reference by someone whom has established credibility with your prospect or customer.

2. *Provide a Level of Confidence in the Certainty of a Positive Outcome.* When prospective buyers have little-to-no experience with a product, service, solution, proposal, or seller, the buyer has no first-hand knowledge of what the post-purchase environment will look like or what the outcome of the

purchase action will be. This gives the buyer pause and makes the proposition a risky one. When the seller can allay the buyer's fears by presenting the buyer with positive examples of where the seller has done the same thing for other buyers (thus establishing credibility), or present the buyer with like-customer references, the seller is acting to increase the buyer's confidence of the likelihood or certainty of a positive outcome, which serves to reduce the buyer's perceived riskiness of a purchase decision.

The "Skepticism" Buying Emotion

In the process of Movement, once a prospective buyer overcomes the Buying Emotion of *fear*, they then become merely skeptical about making a purchase decision. When buyers are *skeptical*, they harbor doubts and unbelief about the promise of the outcome of a purchase decision. As a result, the skeptical buyer is cautious due to such uncertainty and is therefore unwilling to move forward with a purchase until such skepticism is eased.

In sales, a buyer's skepticism is mostly a function of the risk they believe to be inherent in a purchase decision—risk that results from the buyer's lack of knowledge of, experience with and, therefore, outcome-certainty of a purchase, along with their perception of seller's (and therefore, the seller's company's) credibility. Although the skeptical buyer is more trusting and open to making a purchase decision and, eventually, a purchase, than the fearful buyer, the buyer nonetheless maintains reservations about doing so. The skeptical buyer is looking to gain an added degree of comfort by working with a seller whom the buyer believes to be credible; the buyer is looking for someone whom she can trust to make the purchase experience and its associated outcome a positive one.

Because of this need to work with a credible seller and the buyer's heightened awareness of the attributes & characteristics of the sellers by whom she is contacted, the skeptical buyer is on *charlatan watch*, spotting all of the signs of a seller whom the buyer believes does not have her best business interests at heart: (1) never demonstrating a clear understanding of the buyer's interests, objectives, or position, and never bothering to question the buyer in order to gain an understanding; (2) pushing the buyer when the buyer wants to be *led*; (3) spewing endless details and minutiae about their products; (4) no listening, but talking—giving the buyer the impression that the seller doesn't care or have a genuine interest in the buyer's business; (5) disparaging the seller's competitors; (6) never establishing credibility or giving the buyer a reason why she should trust what the seller is saying.

This skeptical buyer does not want to be duped or coerced into making a post-purchase regretful decision by some slick-but-unsubstantial seller (*charlatan*), and the buyer's skepticism puts them on bulls##t alert; unfortunately, far too many sellers cause prospective buyer's bulls##t meters to go off when engaged in the sale.

The point to be understood is that the seller's credibility and empathy (demonstrated through a selling motion that is consultative in nature) play a significant and important role in allaying buyers' fears and unease about making a purchase, even when the buyer may not have any degree of relevant experience with the item being considered for purchase. This is illustrated in the table below.

THE SKEPTICISM BUYING EMOTION

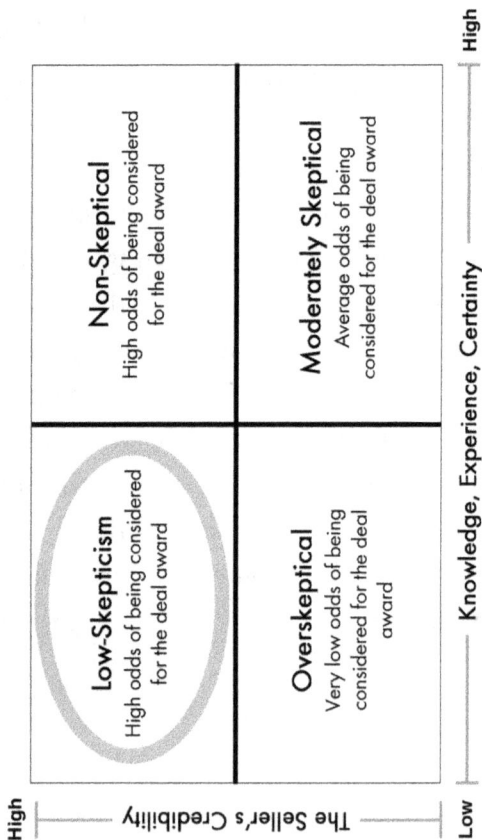

	High
Low-Skepticism High odds of being considered for the deal award	**Non-Skeptical** High odds of being considered for the deal award
Overskeptical Very low odds of being considered for the deal award	**Moderately Skeptical** Average odds of being considered for the deal award

The Seller's Credibility — High / Low

Knowledge, Experience, Certainty — High

The seller's level of credibility with a buyer can mollify the buyer's skepticism about the seller's proposal and increase the seller's chances of gaining a sale

Considerations for helping prospective buyers become less skeptical of making a purchase decision

Skeptical buyers experience many of the same emotions as fearful buyers, and the things that sellers do to allay the fears of the fearful buyer serve to reduce or eliminate the skepticism of the skeptical buyer, namely: establish credibility and provide the buyer with a level of confidence in the certainty of a positive outcome of a purchase decision.

The "Calm & Openness" Buying Emotion

When a buyer is *calm*, the buyer is moving or has completely moved away from pursuing a purchase based on the risk-induced Buying Emotions of *fear* and *skepticism,* and is at least open to considering opportunities for improvement. However, it does not mean that the buyer is open to considering a *specific* seller's recommendations or proposal; it only means the buyer is willing to listen to what the seller is proposing and to work with the seller on providing those things (such as data or the company's publicly-announced business plans, for example) the seller needs in order to provide the buyer with a better understanding of how the seller can possibly help. The calm & open prospective buyer is also willing and interested to learn, since they are not as fearful about making a purchase with a specific buyer or skeptical about some aspect of the purchase: the downside risk, the seller, the product, the value, or other concerns.

When a prospective buyer achieves a sense of calm with working with a specific seller, the buyer is signaling that she is open to the possibility of pursuing an initiative and has found someone whom she believes can help her make a "good" purchase decision; someone whom she believes is a safe choice to work with toward achieving her business objectives and the desired outcome(s) of the purchase-related initiative. While this stage of Buyer Movement—from *fear*-to-*skepticism*, from *skepticism*-to-*calm & openness*—does not ensure that the buyer will find the seller's proposal attractive or even viable, it does signal that the buyer has granted the seller permission to move forward with the sales process. This is the KEY stage of Buyer Movement because it is the first time in the sales cycle that a fearful prospective buyer is willing to engage with a seller toward the possibility of a closed sale. Skeptical buyers do not suddenly open themselves up to new ideas or different ways of doing things without first removing their restrictive barrier of skepticism and *allowing themselves to be sold to.* This is the major characteristic of the *calm & openness* Buying Emotion: the prospective buyer will open herself up to the possibility of making a purchase decision and let her guard down so that a seller can demonstrate her credibility, her willingness to support the buyer, and her interest in helping the buyer accomplish the buyer's business objectives more so than she is interested in selling her a product.

> In practice, we know that most sellers have more of an interest in selling their wares—so that they can earn commissions, make lots of money, and keep their jobs—than they do in helping buyers do *their* jobs. However, the long-term successful sellers know that the two go hand-in-hand—they cannot make lots of money without helping buyers accomplish their business objectives—and they also know how to give prospective buyers this impression whether they are sincere about it or not.

The "Interest" Buying Emotion

Imagine one day you walk into a clothing store. Upon entering the store you are greeted by that typical breed of mall-hired hipster salesperson who yells, "Hey! Whatcha buyin' today?" Before entering the store you heard rumors about how some people who patronized the clothing store felt ripped-off afterward because they believed the store overcharged them for the clothing items they purchased. And since you have no experience with this store or knowledge about how they really operate, you believe there is risk associated with making a purchase in the store and, as a result, you are fearful about doing so.

"What can I help you with today?" the perky salesperson asks, "Nothing. I'm just browsing," you reply. At that point you see a tee-shirt that you are really interested in buying. The price: $50. "Damn!" you exclaim within earshot of the salesperson, who assures you that $50 is a fair price for that designer tee-shirt. The salesperson pulls out a stack of newspaper circulars and shows you several websites offering the same tee-shirt for sale at prices ranging from $49.99 to $55. Those actions by the seller eased your fear of making a purchase in the store (because, based on the rumors, you believed you would be ripped-off on price), but because you had no first-hand experience with the store and the overly-shadowing salesperson made you uncomfortable, you remained skeptical about patronizing the store.

At that point, a couple of friends of yours see you in the store and come in to say hello. The friends tell you that they often shop in the store and have never had a bad shopping experience there. Now, with these testimonials based on first-hand experience (*references*), your skepticism is eased and you are now willing to openly browse the store to see if there is anything you would like to purchase; you have moved from the Buying Emotions of *fear* and *skepticism*, to *calm & openness*. And now that you are calm and have opened yourself up to the possibility of making a purchase, you will allow yourself to become *interested* in purchasing any clothing items that meet your shopping requirements.

A buyer will usually not become interested in any specific purchase or open to the idea of purchasing *your* proposition until they have overcome their fear of making a purchase decision, their skepticism about the value of making a purchase, consider the possibility of a purchase decision with a sense of calm, and become interested and open to the idea of actually purchasing something. Once a prospective buyer is open to making a purchase and is convinced that there are viable options available to help her accomplish her business (or personal business-related) objectives, the buyer will then actively engage in the process of deciding what to purchase.

Interest and Buyer Objections

When prospective buyers are moved from the position of calm & openness, to the possibility of a purchase decision, to the position of general interest in pursuing a solution to a problem, they begin to feel that they should learn more about the seller and the seller's products, services, solutions, company capabilities, or overall proposal. It is at this point in the sales cycle that prospective buyers *really* start to ask questions and express concerns (i.e. raise objection) about the seller's proposal. If the seller is to continue to move the buyer through the Buying Emotions toward a sale, the seller will have to give the buyer the added degree of comfort with and confidence in the seller and the seller's proposal by assuaging *all* of the buyer's concerns and satisfactorily addressing *all* of the buyer's objections. Objection handling is such a critical aspect of Buyer Movement that I will expound on it here.

The Nature of Objections

An *objection* is the prospective buyer's way of telling the seller that something about the seller's proposal is giving the buyer pause and—until the issue is resolved to the buyer's satisfaction—the buyer will not go forward with the process. Prospects and existing customers alike raise objections for many different reasons, including (but not limited to):

- The seller has not effectively demonstrated the value of the product, service, solution, or proposal to the buyer and the buyer doesn't see the value in it.

- The buyer doesn't trust the seller.

- The buyer really does not want to make the purchase or do the deal but the seller is unaware of that fact.

- The buyer is skeptical and is not totally comfortable with the proposal.

- A competitor's proposal is more attractive to the buyer than the seller's.

Whatever the reason for the objection the fact remains: the prospective buyer has placed a barrier between herself and the seller's desired sales outcome (the deal), and until the barrier / objection has been satisfactorily overcome, the seller will be unable to move the sales process forward to close the deal. Given this reality, it stands to reason that the first thing a seller must do when a buyer raises an objection is to understand the cause of the objection or concern, and to uncover the "real" issue(s) that underlie the concern. It will be very difficult to close a deal until the buyer's *real* issues are addressed to the buyer's satisfaction.

Objections are hurdles—literally and figuratively: the runner cannot attempt to cross the second hurdle until the first hurdle has been cleared. And if the runner does not successfully clear each hurdle, the odds of the runner winning the race are low. In the case of the sales deal pursuit process, the seller must clear *all* hurdles (satisfactorily address every buyer objection) or risk leaving the buyer with unaddressed issues that create doubt in the buyer's mind about the goodness of the seller and his or her proposal, and the potential risk of making the purchase decision with that seller.

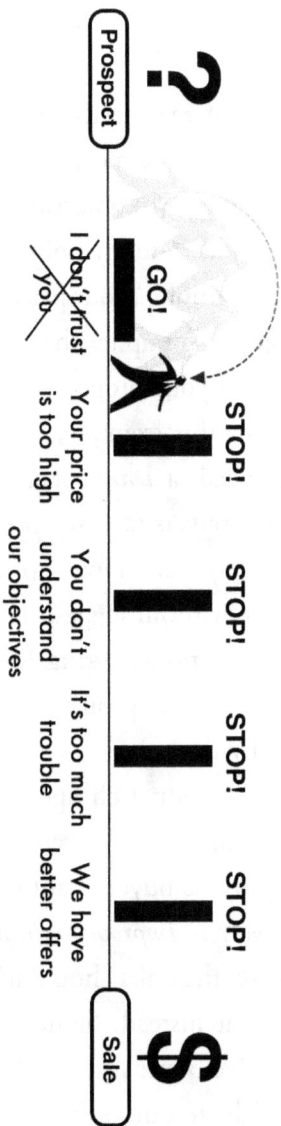

BUYER MOVEMENT BEYOND THE BARIERS

Each **objection** raised is a barrier (hurdle) preventing the seller from moving the sales engagement forward

"Real" Need vs. "Perceived" Need:
The *Price* Objection

To explain the concept of *real* needs versus *wants* versus perceived *needs*, I will use the most common objection raised by buyers—the *price* objection—as the example through which to illustrate my point.

When a buyer says, for example, "Your prices are too high," the statement (objection) implies that the buyer is unhappy with the price of your proposal and wants a lower price from you. In this example, is a "lower price" the *real* customer need, a *want,* or a *perceived need?* In other words, when buyers raise the *price objection*, do they really, ultimately want a lower price from the seller? The conventional wisdom suggests not often.

As with many initial objections, asking for a lower price is a symptom of something bigger the buyer wants. Think about it: why do buyers ask for a lower price? Answer: To buy the product cheaper. Why do buyers want to buy things cheaper? Answer: to reduce costs and expenses. And why do buyers want to reduce costs and expenses? Answer: *To improve profit margins!* Knowing this to be the case, the seller should not focus on lowering their prices but instead, figure out ways they can help the prospective buyer improve her company's profits (given all of the resources available to the seller through their company and affiliates). **The best sellers will re-focus the buyer on ways the seller can help the buyer improve profits (the *real* need) as opposed to fighting to get a lower price (the *perceived* need).**

There are several price-based realities the every seller must acknowledge:

1. You will *always* get price objections from prospects and customers; price objections will not go away.

2. Someone will always have a lower price than yours, so learn how to sell against it.

3. You will lose some business to a lower-price proposal. Know when to cut your losses and focus on the deals you can win.

4. It is not unreasonable to believe that 40% of *commodity* product purchase decisions are, indeed, made based on the lowest price. In other categories, that estimate is approximately 15% of purchase decisions. That means between 60 and 85% of purchase decisions ate NOT based solely on price; win those deals.

5. Selling against a lower price can be challenging, but not impossible.

The Burning Question

Over the past 25 years, I have worked with professional sellers of all stripes and experience levels. And regardless of the company, the industry, the country, or the size of the business, I was guaranteed to cross paths with lots of sellers who use the age-old excuse of "The competitor's price was lower," as the reason why they lost a deal. If having the lowest price is the only way a seller can sell a product, then why does the company need *the seller* when they can simply print pricing sheets and send the sheets to customers? This begs the question: *What differentiates the "can't sell against lower prices" seller from a pricing sheet?* Or consider this: Assume two commodity products you are contemplating purchasing are exactly the same, and one seller lowers its price, making it less expensive than the other seller's product. In this scenario, what are the reasons you would still buy the higher-priced item? Use the space provided below to write some answers to these two questions presented in the table.

What differentiates a sales rep from a pricing sheet?	What are the reasons you would still buy a commodity product from *Seller A* when *Seller B* has the exact same product for a lower price?

The answers to these questions will give you insight into the things needed to help overcome price objections. This is what we, as sellers, have to think about and integrate into our selling motions when selling against a lower-price competitor and when buyers raise the price objection. Buyers will pay more for one fungible product over another if they feel *the purchase is worth the added price.* And what makes a more expensive purchase "worth it" for buyers? Value.

What is "value"? In the most simplistic terms, *value* is whatever the buyer says it is. Sellers cannot dictate to a buyer what is valuable and what is not. Value is like "beauty," it is in the eye of the beholder. Unlike *beauty,* however, in the business setting there are various ways to articulate and consider the value delivered by a seller or a company. Consider a furniture manufacturer. The company buys raw materials and components, then processes and assembles them into finished products. The finished goods are then sold to customers. The furniture manufacturer added value to the raw materials it brought in. The company's value added is the difference between the cost of the raw materials and the price that buyers paid for the furniture.

For sellers, an easier way to understand your value to a buyer or an account is to consider your answers to the following questions:

- If my customer was presented with my apple and the exact same apple from my competitor for the exact same price, and the customer decided to purchase the apple from *me*, why did the customer do it?

- If I managed a major account for 5 years and after that five-year period, another sales rep took over the management of my account and continued to get the same sales volume from the account that I did, then did I provide any differentiating value to that account?

When I conduct workshops and the issue of *value* is raised, I ask the participants to answer the following questions in an effort to understand the value they and their company provide to customers:

- If you or your company went away today, who would care and why?

- What is the difference between your accounts with you (or your company) and your accounts without you (or your company)?

Understanding and being able to articulate your and your company's value to a buyer when responding to challenging objections (especially the price objection) can go a long way toward establishing (or reinforcing) credibility and helping the buyer understand why doing business with you is in their best interest.

Responding to Objections:
The 4 Ps of Objection Handling

Any conversation about buyer objections would be incomplete without offering best practices for responding effectively to objections. The best approach for responding to and handling objections—an approach we teach at The Water Training Institute—is to execute The Water Method's *4 Ps of Objection Handling*:

1. *Predict the objections*: One of the benefits of pre-call planning is the anticipation of the objections the buyer is likely to raise during the meeting, and preparing responses to each of the anticipated objections. During the call planning process, we at The Water Training Institute ask sellers to think of five objections they believe the prospective buyer will raise during the planned meeting. This activity is a valuable practice that can contribute to a productive meeting with a buyer.

2. *Prepare for the objections.* For each objection that the seller anticipates the buyer to raise during the meeting for which the seller is preparing, the seller

(and his or her sales team) should prepare responses to each of the objections just in case the prospective buyer does raise them. Satisfactorily addressing a buyer's objections can help the seller establish credibility with the buyer, making it easier to move the buyer toward a sale. Conversely, when a seller cannot satisfactorily address each of the buyer's objections, the seller seems unprepared, incompetent, and risks damaging his or her credibility with the buyer.

3. *Preempt the objections.* When the seller has determined the objections that a buyer is likely to raise in a meeting, the seller can then go the extra mile and not only prepare a response to each of the anticipated objections, but also forestall the objections—where possible—from ever being raised. If, for example, the seller anticipates that the prospective buyer will express a concern that no one the buyer is aware of is using the proposed product and the buyer doesn't want to be the guinea pigs for a new product, the seller can prepare customer references from other clients that are using the product in question successfully, and present the references to the buyer before the buyer can raise the objection. The seller can also present the rebuttals to the

THE ART *of* MOVEMENT

anticipated objections prior to the buyer raising them in the meeting.

4. *Present a response to the objections.* At some point during the meeting the seller will present the prepared responses to the anticipated objections. If the objection responses are presented *after* the buyer has raised the objection in the meeting, the seller should follow the fundamental objection handling best practice (see the next paragraph below) and effortlessly deliver the prepared responses as appropriate.

Any recommendations for responding to objections would be incomplete without consideration of following the fundamental objection handling best practices of listening, empathizing, questioning for clarification, and addressing the objection satisfactorily. Believe it or not, most sellers fail to follow this basic-yet-proven-effective approach for responding to customer objections. An abbreviated outline of the approach is provided below.

Listen and Empathize. Buyers raise objections because they are somehow not satisfied with the seller's proposal or proposition. Oftentimes, when buyers raise objections, they are frustrated and need to vent or be heard—not simply *listened to*. Empathizing with buyers when they raise objections tells them that the seller understands their issues and/or frustrations and that the seller understands why the buyer is dissatisfied. This simple courtesy can move a situation from being confrontational to cordial. When that is accomplished, customers are then willing to engage in a productive discussion.

When sellers fail to acknowledge a buyer's dissatisfaction or frustration and fail to put themselves in the buyer's shoes to understand the buyer's point of view, buyers often become even more dissatisfied because they believe their concerns are falling on deaf ears and that the seller doesn't care about them.

Question for Clarification. Sellers should make the effort to clearly understand both the buyer's perceived objections and what is really behind the objections. Also, sellers should be sure they understand the buyer's objection before they attempt to respond to it. This is easily done by validating your understanding of the objection by asking, " … is my understanding of [your objection] correct?"

Address the Objection and Validate that it has been Resolved. When the seller responds to objections, it is always good to validate with the buyer that the objections have been addressed to their satisfaction and to use this as an opportunity to try to close the deal. For example, the close attempt might go like this: "Have the issues raised been addressed and resolved to your satisfaction? Good. Then, if there are no further issues and you've already agreed that the proposal provides your company with the best financial benefit, then let's move forward …"

The "Action Mode" Buying Emotion

The *action mode* Buying Emotion is what all sales professionals want prospective buyers to experience, for it is in action mode that prospective buyers look to become *actual* buyers and execute a purchase. When prospective buyers experiences the *action* Buying Emotion they—most often subconsciously—engage in the process of making a purchase known as the *Buying Cycle*.

The Buying Cycle

Buying is the process of making a purchase decision. The "Buying Cycle" describes the sequence of stages that a typical buyer goes through when deciding to buy something. The stages include:

1. *Identification of a need* (whether real or perceived) to be satisfied, a goal to be accomplished, or an objec-

tive to be achieved that influences the need to possibly make a purchase.

2. *Investigation of potential solutions* that could satisfy a need, accomplish a goal, and/or achieve an objective.

3. *Evaluation of the alternatives*, either of which could accomplish the defined objective(s) to varying degrees.

4. *Making the purchase decision* and buying something.

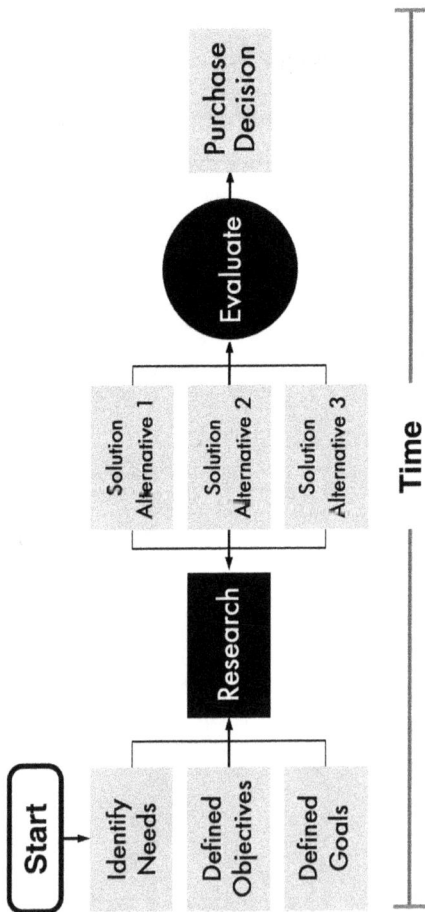

THE BUYING CYCLE

Start → Identify Needs / Defined Objectives / Defined Goals → **Research** → Solution Alternative 1 / Solution Alternative 2 / Solution Alternative 3 → Evaluate → **Purchase Decision**

Time

Shorten the Buying Cycle and improve your odds by engaging with the prospective buyer to shorten the Research, Evaluation, and Purchase Decision processes

The Buying Cycle differs from Buying Emotions in that the Buying Cycle describes *actions taken* on the part of the prospective buyer toward a possible purchase decision, whereas Buying Emotions describe *sentiments that lead to actions or inaction*. For instance, a prospective buyer experiencing the sentiment or emotion to take action (Action Mode) might act out the sentiment by taking the action to make a purchase. So, while the Buying Cycle and Buying Emotions are different concepts entirely, they are aligned, however, as illustrated in the diagram below.

MOVEMENT BEYOND BUYING EMOTIONS
The Buying Cycle Aligned with Buying Emotions

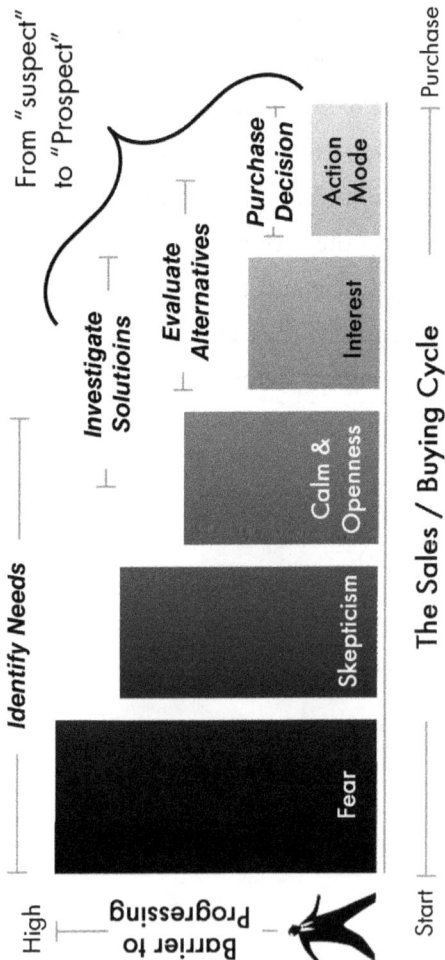

From "suspect"
to "Prospect"

Identify Needs

Investigate Solutioins

Evaluate Alternatives

Purchase Decision

Fear

Skepticism

Calm & Openness

Interest

Action Mode

High

Barrier to Progressing

Start

Purchase

The Sales / Buying Cycle

02

The Art of Movement

What is *Movement*?

To "move" is to change from one position to another; to advance or progress. This is what sellers do as they work with prospective buyers in an effort to sell their wares: they *move* or *change* the prospective buyer from an initial position of fear & uncertainty to a position of interest & action as they *advance* down the sales cycle toward a closed deal and a signed contract. Based on this notion, as I wrote in the *Introduction*, I describe selling as *The Art of Movement*. It is the art of taking a person from some undesirable initial position or mindset and *moving* them to a position where they share your vision and accept your recommendation because they believe it to be in their best interest—business, professional, or personal.

MOVEMENT
From Fear & Uncertainty to a Purchase Action

Fear and Uncertainty	The Selling Motion	The Desired Action

The Four Stages of Buyer Movement

Buyer Movement is the act of moving a prospective buyer through the progression of Buying Emotions that buyers often experience when contemplating making a purchase. It is the process of moving prospective buyers from:

- **Stage 1**: Fear to Skepticism
- **Stage 2**: Skepticism to Calm & Openness
- **Stage 3**: Calm & Openness to Interest
- **Stage 4**: Interest to Action Mode

THE 4 STAGES of BUYER MOVEMENT

And the Relative Magnitude of their Barrier to Gaining a Sale

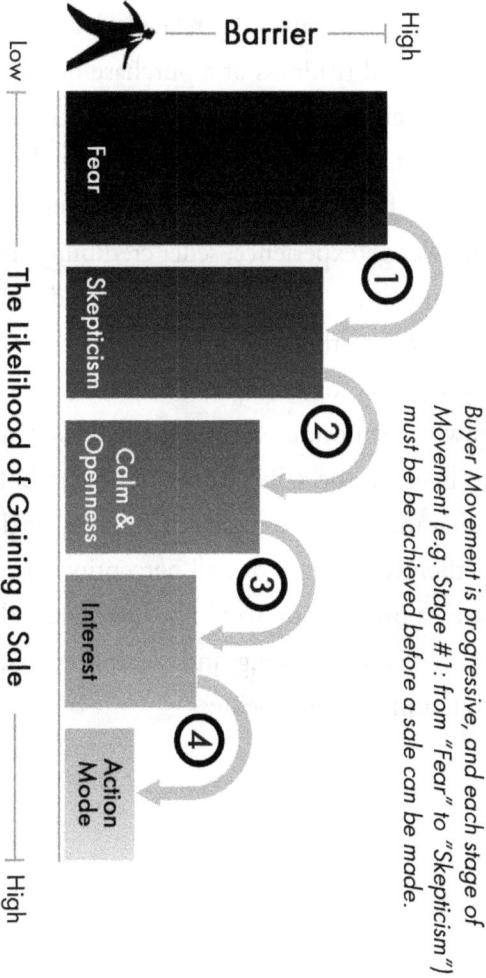

Barrier — High

Low

High

Fear

Skepticism ①

Calm & Openness ②

Interest ③

Action Mode ④

The Likelihood of Gaining a Sale

Buyer Movement is progressive, and each stage of Movement (e.g. Stage #1: from "Fear" to "Skepticism") must be be achieved before a sale can be made.

The Necessity of Movement in a Sale

The odds of closing a sale or being considered as a viable candidate for a sale are conversely related to a buyer's *fear* and the perceived riskiness of a purchase decision: the lower the buyer's fear of making a purchase, the higher the seller's chances of selling a proposal to them. The combination of the three impacts on a buyer's *fear* emotion—knowledge/experience, seller credibility, and risk impact—contribute to the overall perceived riskiness of a purchase and the associated unattractiveness of that proposition. If, for example, a buyer has a high degree of knowledge about a product being considered for purchase, believes the seller to be highly-credible, and believes that the negative impact of making the decision is low, then the buyer's overall perception of the riskiness of such a proposition would be low, giving the seller a great chance of winning and closing the sale. This is illustrated in the table below.

IMPACTS ON THE FEAR EMOTION
And Their Contribution to the Perceived Risk of a Purchase

RISK / FEAR	Knowledge, Experience, Certainty	The Seller's Credibility	The Impact of Failure
Low	High	High	Low
	High	Low	Low
	Low	High	Low
	High	High	High
Medium	Low	High	High
	High	Low	High
High	Low	Low	High
	Low	Low	Low

If the seller cannot *move* the prospective buyer away from his emotion of *fear* and the associated perceived riskiness of making a purchase action—barring some external influence on the prospective buyer—the seller will never win that sale with that buyer. Period. If the seller is unsuccessful at moving the prospective buyer away from his emotion of *skepticism*—barring some external influence on the prospective buyer—the seller will probably never win that sale with that buyer. If the seller is successful at allaying the buyer's skepticism and moving the buyer to a position of calm & openness, only at that point will the seller have gained a *prospect*, whereas previously, the seller was dealing with a *suspect*. But even at this point in the process of Buyer Movement the seller cannot become comfortable that a sale is imminent. It's not enough to move the prospective buyer to become open to *considering* the prospect of making a purchase to address some issue or achieve some objective, the seller must continue to move the prospective buyer from merely being *open* to the idea of a purchase to being *interested* in the *seller's* proposition as a (if not *thee*) viable alternative to addressing the buyer's issue. The reason is because—until a prospective buyer considers the seller's specific proposal as a viable candidate for purchase—the seller has simply created a general interest on the buyer's part and not a specific interest in the seller's proposition.

Selling as *Art* vs. *Science* vs. *Process*

Opinions abound from experts, consultants, and even the average salesperson on whether selling is an *art*, a *science*, a *process*, or something altogether different. Some argue that the sales process needs to become more of a science than an art. Effective sales execution, they argue, is driven by data, other inputs, and tools that allow companies to assess the marketplace, determine which outlets are most valuable in a market, which products to target within the outlets in a region, and how to measure execution. This data-driven targeted approach to sales execution is, to some, more *science* than *art*.

Others believe that sales is a *process*; a process that starts with a prospective buyer, then moves to the stage of understanding the prospect's requirements & business objectives, then moves to the solution development stage, and ends with a sale. While I agree that the act of selling does typically follow a series of activities that are so commonly-executed they can be (and are) considered a standard *process*—research supports this—I more strongly believe that describing sales as *simply* a process that one follows to get from "A" to "B" ignores the nuances of moving a prospective buyer to a sale as well as the fact that many sales get done in unconventional ways without following a script or a process. In addition, it's an insult to those sellers who use their guile and experience to win business as often as they follow any sales process. That being said, I have no qualms with the Stages to the Sale being considered a process; in many ways, it is.

I describe selling is an *art* for the following reason: When the selling motion that begins with a reluctant prospective buyer is executed to such a degree that the once-reluctant prospect shifts and ultimately agrees that the seller's proposition is valuable and is moved to make a purchase, the end-to-end activity is of more than ordinary significance and holds an appeal and even a form of beauty at its core. The skillful *movement* of a prospective buyer from no interest to a sale requires creativity, imagination, and often a natural talent that embodies artistic expression when executed properly. Yes, selling can be artistic when movement is executed skillfully, just as a dancer's refined movements, Magnus Carlsen's chess strategies, and martial *artist* Bruce Lee's katas are considered beautiful and artistic.

03

The Five Sales-Forces
That Create Movement

I n the previous chapter I discussed the necessity for a
sales professional to create *movement* in a prospective
buyer, moving them from the Buyer Emotions of fear,
skepticism, and closed-mindedness, to the position of
being interested in the seller's proposition as a viable
candidate for purchase. But what creates movement?
What makes objects or people *move*? In physics, motion is a change in position with respect to time and a
reference point. Prospective buyers, just like inanimate
objects, don't move on their own. Motion requires an
applied *force* to cause that movement (as long as there is
no other counter force to challenge it) as Isaac Newton
(a 17th century scientist) described in his first law of

motion. Force is the power to influence behavior, affect change, or control a circumstance. It is the ability to move a prospective buyer from a lack of interest to making a purchase decision in the seller's favor.

But what creates the force that causes movement? Specifically, what creates *sales-force*, which I define as the ability of a seller to cause change in a prospective buyer's opinion of the value that the seller and his or her proposition holds? It is the seller's ability to move a prospective buyer down the path of Buying Emotions from *fear* to *action mode*, culminating in the purchase of the seller's proposal. With that as the definition of *sales-force*, there are five specific sales competencies that create the force which causes movement in a prospective buyer and contribute greatest to long-term sustained success. I refer to these sales competencies as *The Five Sales-Forces*.

Research: Sustained Sales Success

To understand the characteristic of sellers who (1) consistently won complex deals based on their ability to apply sales-force and move prospective buyers to a sale, and (2) had sustained sales success over an "extended period of time" (5 years or greater), I analyzed sales data from the sales engagements of 182 sales professionals between 1987 and 2014 across various industries and with varied levels of selling tenure and experience. In addition, I used the sales performance data from more than 1,500 sales professionals that my colleagues and I have trained, coached, managed, and developed since 2005, and I interviewed more than 220 professional sellers in an effort to identify the traits and characteristics of the sellers who had the most sustained success over time and the sellers who had the least success.

Before I can begin a discussion of the characteristics of the most "successful" sellers, we must not only define the determinants of being a "successful" and "unsuccessful" seller, but we must also define "sustained" sales "success" and assure consistency in the success criteria when evaluating the performance of professional sellers. What I mean by *consistency* is ensuring that the sales success criteria used—such as quota-attainment percentage, for instance—are common among sellers so that we compare apples-to-apples, and that sellers with uncommon success criteria—such as *time available to take painting lessons*—are excluded.

Trying to establish a reasonable and consistently-applied set of criteria to use for determining whether a seller is "good," "bad," "successful," "unsuccessful," or even "serviceable" is difficult. To me, it's like trying to determine which school teacher within a state is *deservedly* the Teacher of the Year. Every year I see on television or in the news that some frail, senior American woman from some small town with a population less than that of a Football Bowl Subdivision / FBS (Division I-A) college football team is named Teacher of the Year. The news story goes on to say how her students love her and she is everyone's favorite teacher because she is so nice—almost like a grandmother. My first question when I see such an announcement is: of the 956,000 High School teachers in America how did this ONE end up being the Teacher of the Year; what were the criteria? Did the voters apply the same criteria to the other 955,999 teachers and she happened to bubble to the top of the list? Did they use percentage test-grade increase year-to-year as a measure? Did they use *likeability*—whatever that means? Did they use the greatest percentage of inner-city poverty-stricken single-parent-raised malnourished illiterate children to be brought up from the 10th to the 90th percentile in reading comprehension? *How did they decide*!? Would that Teacher of the Year be as effective teaching underprivileged, hard-living High School students in the city of Detroit as she was teaching the students—all of whom she has known since they were born—in her small, upper-middle class town? My guess? She seemed "nice."

As you can imagine there are literally tens if not hundreds of criteria that companies use to determine whether or not their sellers have had "successful" years. The most common metric is *sales percent-to-goal.* After all, from the company's perspective, they hired the sellers to go out and sell stuff in amounts that exceed their assigned dollar goals. Conversely, some companies do not assign sales goals or quotas to their sales reps at all, and their "success" measures include such things as *the percentage of prospects moved through the sales funnel to a sales win.* This should give you an indication of just how difficult it is to define a singular measure or set of criteria that define a seller's "success" across a disparate body of sellers, since the determinants of sales success are company-specific. That being the case, it is possible to study and measure various financial metrics (such as income growth over a period of years), experiences sellers have gained, and activities in which the sellers engage—metrics, experiences, and activities that correlate with the designated "sales leaders" within companies. I believe the *Sustained Sales Success Criteria* I developed based on my research, in addition to the experience in coaching and developing sales professionals for more than 25 years by my sales colleagues and me, combine to provide what I believe is a reliable approach for determining the characteristics of the most productive, sustaining, consistent, overachieving sellers; in other words, *successful* sellers over time.

Sustained Sales Success Criteria

- Sales as a percent to quota or goal.
- Number of years (out of a minimum of 5) the sales goal was attained, understanding that various factors can affect quota attainment, not the least of which is poor quota setting.
- Number of "different sales experiences" obtained during a career and the relationship to goal attainment. Varied experiences contribute to sales effectiveness and skills improvement.
- Sales acumen and skill mastery.
- Percent of deals closed with senior managers (e.g. C-Level executives).
- Percent of opportunities moved from "Level 1" (lead or suspect) in the sales funnel to "Level 5" (sales win and signed contract).

  - *Level 1*: Lead, Suspect. An anything goes assortment of unqualified potential sales targets usually generated from a marketing lead-generation campaign.

- *Level 2*: Prospect. The leads have been sorted to identify those suspects that meet some targeting or pursuit criteria.

- *Level 3*: Qualify. The list of prospects has been narrowed based on those prospects that meet the company's or the sales team's qualification criteria, meaning there is a higher likelihood that these qualified targets offer the prospects of a real sales opportunity.

- *Level 4*: Proposal. The qualified targets that progressed through the sales cycle and warranted the submission of a proposal for services.

- *Level 5*: Close. The number of prospects that signed a purchase contract.

- Income growth year-over-year.
- Average sales job tenure in with a company.
- Risk acceptance.
- The annual number of hours spent on sales skill development.
- Percent of customer meeting objectives achieved.
- Account Planning acumen and execution.

Taking these criteria into consideration, the results of my analysis revealed the following about the most productive (how well one produces intended results) and effective (producing intended results) sellers, and those that were less productive and effective.

Findings on Sustained Sales Success		
Characteristic	The Most Effective, Productive Sellers	The Least Effective, Productive Sellers
Sales as a percent to quota or goal	Attained annual sales goals (although some were administered quarterly) in consecutive years. Achieved an average percent-to-goal of 136% for at least 5 consecutive years.	Attained annual sales goals, however, not in all years consecutively. Achieved an average percent-to-goal of 88% for at least 5 consecutive years (some sell in this group had less than 5 years of experience).
Number of years (out of a minimum of 5) the sales goal was attained	5 years	2.6 years (average across the measurement group)
Number of "different sales experiences" obtained	The average seller in this group had an average of 12 years of selling experience working for an average of 3 different companies selling in an average of 2 different industries.	Had an average of 7 years of selling experience across 2 companies working in one industry.
Sales acumen and skill mastery	Mastered or are at least "highly-skilled" at executing the selling fundamentals.	Inconsistent skill levels of executing the selling fundamentals. Ineffective at some of the basic sales skills, especially objection handling and financial selling.

Percent of deals closed through senior managers	68% of the deals won involved at least one meeting with a senior manager (Vice President-level or above) related to the initiative. This varied by the buyers' company size.	36% of the deals won involved at least one meeting with a senior manager (Director-level or above) related to the initiative. This group's selling efforts were primarily directed to manager-level buyers. This varied by the buyers' company size.
Percent of opportunities moved from "Level 1" (lead or suspect) in the sales funnel to "Level 5" (sales win and signed contract).	55%	39%
Personal income growth year-over-year (excluding company-provided merit increases/ raises)	13%	9%
Average sales job tenure in the with the same company	5 years, 2 months	7 years, 6 months
Forecast accuracy	Won 80% of the deals in the pipeline that reached 75% or greater odds of closing.	Won 55% of the deals in the pipeline that reached 75% or greater odds of closing.
The annual number of hours spent on sales skill development	An average of 38 hours per year	An average of 20 hours per year

Percent of customer meeting objectives achieved	This group achieved an average of 81% of the meeting objectives defined prior to the meeting for which a call plan was developed. Prepared call plans for 86% of "significant" meetings.	This group achieved an average of 74% of the meeting objectives defined prior to the meeting for which a call plan was developed. Prepared call plans for 20% of "significant" meetings.
Account Planning acumen and execution	Developed and managed account plans for 82% of accounts that were identified to generate the revenue to achieve annual sales goals.	Developed and managed account plans for 22% of accounts that were identified to generate the revenue to achieve annual sales goals.

During my analysis, I also compiled some revealing data—based on a sales force analysis I conducted for a *Fortune*® 25 corporation in addition to other information—that shed some additional light on why some sellers were less effective than others and, therefore, less successful than others. Due to the nature of the study and the straightforwardness of the findings, I am able to present this compilation of data concisely so that it is easily absorbed, understood, and shared. In general, I was able to develop a broad definition and measure of sales "effectiveness" as well as that of "customer engagement," two categories whose measurable data provided me with great insight into things that sellers and companies can do immediately to improve the sales performance of its sellers.

- **Sales Effectiveness**: The seller's ability to navigate the sales cycle and execute the Stages to the Sale in the shortest amount of time possible. The seller's consistency and skillfulness with Territory Management (including Account Planning). The seller's overall performance: the manner of efficiency—speed through the sales cycle and cost-per-order-dollar—with which the seller's purpose is fulfilled. *I have included a sample list of sales effectiveness metrics in the Appendix of this book.*

- **Customer Engagement**: The seller's ability to articulate and demonstrate the *value* they bring to their customers. The ability to retain customers. The customer satisfaction ratings sellers received. The seller's ability to get initiatives accomplished with their customers. The seller's ability to attract customers to company events.

The major finding from this analysis was the revelation of supporting data that show the correlation between effective customer engagement (meaning: engaging with the customer during each interaction to successfully move the sales process forward), the sales revenue the seller gained from the customer, and the customer retention rate. The data also showed a correlation between sellers' effectiveness and Territory Management, specifically, managing the amount of time spent on non-selling activities. These "non-selling" activities are what I refer to as "Sales Detractors."

Sales detractors are activities in which sellers engage that do not advance the sales process. The more time spent on sales detractors, the less time (available to be) spent on selling activities that lead to a closed deal, and, consequently, the less revenue generated from customers and the lower the customer-retention rate. The list of sales detractors I identified during my sales force analysis of the *Fortune®* 25 corporation and other research includes:

- Managing e-mail
- Reporting & paperwork
- Using sales tools
- Conference calls / sales meetings
- Handling A/R and credit issues
- Duplication of effort
- Completing duplicate requests
- Technical issues
- Travel ("windshield time")
- Customer service-related activities
- "Useless" training
- Handling pricing and contract issues

These data, as well as the correlation between customer engagement, sales detractors, and revenue, are illustrated in the diagram below.

CORRELATION BETWEEN
Productive Customer Engagement and Sales Revenue

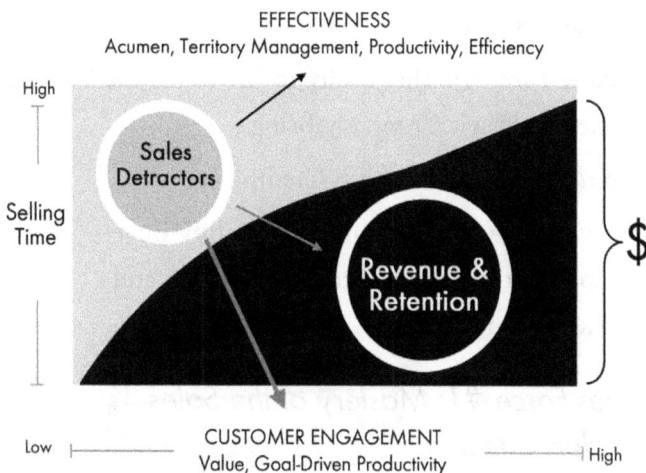

EFFECTIVENESS
Acumen, Territory Management, Productivity, Efficiency

High

Sales
Detractors

Selling
Time

Revenue &
Retention

$

Low

CUSTOMER ENGAGEMENT
Value, Goal-Driven Productivity

High

"**Sales Detractors**" reduce selling time, negatively impacting productive customer engagement, effectiveness, revenue, and retention

As I share in the ensuing paragraphs, through my research and analysis there emerged definitive characteristics of the sellers who had long-term sustained success as well as those sellers who had not. These definitive characteristics create sales-force and Buyer Movement, characteristics that I refer to as *The Five Sales-Forces* that create movement.

The Five Sales-Forces

- *Sales-Force #1*: Mastery of the Sales Fundamentals
- *Sales-Force #2*: The Ability to Build a Financial Business Case
- *Sales-Force #3*: The Ability to Articulate the Value they and their Company Bring
- *Sales-Force #4*: Establish Credibility
- *Sales-Force #5*: The Ability to Mollify Buyers' Constrictive Buying-Emotions of Fear and Skepticism

Sales-Force #1: Mastery of the Sales Fundamentals

The data revealed that the primary determinant of seller effectiveness, productivity, and success over time is a seller's mastery and execution of the fundamentals of selling. Specifically, there are five sales fundamentals that the best performers have mastered and continue to execute in their sales engagements:

- *Listening and questioning for understanding.* This includes extracting, documenting, and validating buyers' requirements and articulating & validating buyers' business objectives.

- *Objection handling.* As documented previously, the seller's ability to satisfactorily address buyers' concerns and objections, then, use the objection as a springboard to a trial close, can significantly enhance a seller's credibility with the buyer.

- *Qualifying and closing; asking for the business.* Ineffective sellers waste lots of time pursuing unqualified opportunities, and even when these sellers do qualify a prospective buyer to verify that the opportunity is real, the ineffective sellers neglect to qualify the customer as a means of bringing the sale to a positive close. These sellers infrequently ask buyers for the business. The best sellers, however, have mastered the skill of qualify-and-close, where the seller not only qualifies that an opportunity is worth pursuing, but also ask for the business during the qualification process.

- *Being forthright, open, & honest.* The best sellers are always forthright and brutally honest with buyers, even when the news they have to share is bad. In addition, these sellers are not afraid to challenge buyers (diplomatically) when the buyer is wrong about an issue. Customers appreciate this level of discourse, and the sellers know it; it puts the seller on equal footing with the buyer which helps establish credibility.

- *Understanding and navigating the sales cycle following the Stages to the Sale.* Believe it or not, the Stages to the Sale in particular, and the sales cycle in general, are fundamental sales concepts that have somehow taken on the appearance of being something complex and impossible to execute; they're not. The successful sellers have imbedded an understanding of the Stages to the Sale into their natural selling motion and unconsciously (on *autopilot*) execute the Stages to the Sale as they pursue sales opportunities. This intuitive ability to effectively navigate the sales cycle, it appears, comes with experience over time as depicted in the chart below under *Stage 4* of the Sales Experience Cycle.

SALES EXPERIENCE CYCLE

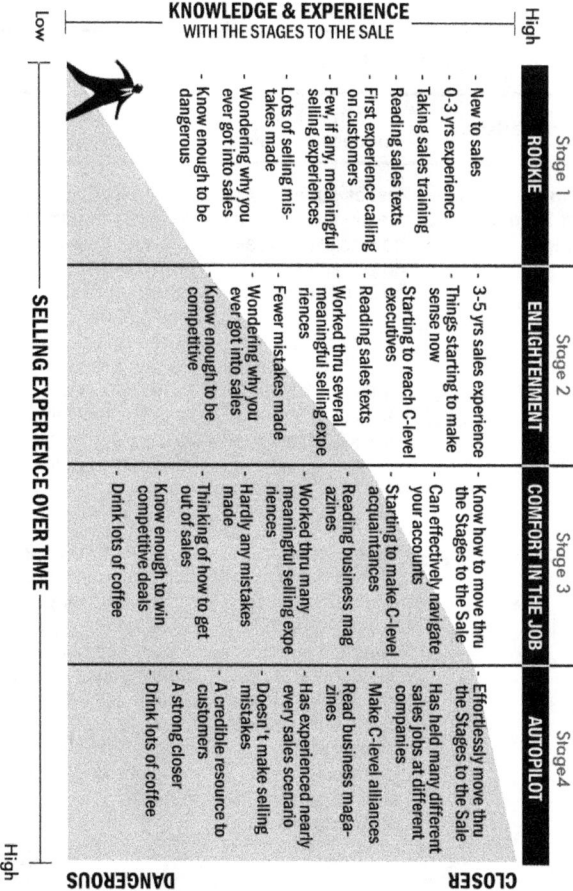

KNOWLEDGE & EXPERIENCE
WITH THE STAGES TO THE SALE — Low / High

Stage 1 ROOKIE	Stage 2 ENLIGHTENMENT	Stage 3 COMFORT IN THE JOB	Stage 4 AUTOPILOT
- New to sales	- 3-5 yrs sales experience	- Know how to move thru the Stages to the Sale	- Effortlessly move thru the Stages to the Sale
- 0-3 yrs experience	- Things starting to make sense now	- Can effectively navigate your accounts	- Has held many different sales jobs at different companies
- Taking sales training	- Starting to reach C-level executives	- Starting to make C-level acquaintances	- Make C-level alliances
- Reading sales texts	- Reading sales texts	- Reading business magazines	- Read business magazines
- First experience calling on customers	- Worked thru several meaningful selling experiences	- Worked thru many meaningful selling experiences	- Has experienced nearly every sales scenario
- Few, if any, meaningful selling experiences	- Fewer mistakes made	- Hardly any mistakes made	- Doesn't make selling mistakes
- Lots of selling mistakes made	- Wondering why you ever got into sales	- Thinking of how to get out of sales	- A credible resource to customers
- Wondering why you ever got into sales	- Know enough to be competitive	- Know enough to win competitive deals	- A strong closer
- Know enough to be dangerous		- Drink lots of coffee	- Drink lots of coffee

SELLING EXPERIENCE OVER TIME — Low / High

ROOKIE — DANGEROUS — CLOSER

89

A comparison between the most successful sellers and the least successful sellers related to their *mastery of the sales fundamentals* is provided in the table below.

Mastery of Sales Fundamentals

Characteristic	The Most Successful Sellers	The Least Successful Sellers
Listening and questioning for understanding	Posses superior questioning skills and the discipline to listen more than speak during initial customer meetings. Adept at extracting business requirements, validating them, and re-articulating them as business objectives.	Have a tendency to dominate the discussion with their verbosity. Ineffective at extracting customer requirements. Rarely, if ever, re-articulates the customers' requirements as business objectives. Fails to learn what's important to customers.
Objection Handling	Prepare for and, where possible, preempt objections from being raised. Follow the basic objection-handling routine (listen, empathize, clarify, validate, address, verify). Use the objection-handling process to qualify and close the buyer.	Does not follow basic objection handling routines. Never prepares for objections. Never uses objection handling as a *qualify & close* opportunity. Often debates buyers over the buyers' concerns and frustrations.

Qualifying and closing; asking for the business	The successful seller is a strong closer who uses the trial-close at every opportunity. This seller does not pursue unqualified opportunities and continually qualifies toward the close in every engagement.	The least successful seller lacks confidence to ask buyers for the business straightforwardly, even when they have justified their proposal.
Being forthright, open, & honest	The most successful sellers foster a professional, peer-level relationship with their customers. This includes having mutually-respectful candid conversations and honest discussions about business opportunities. These sellers are not subservient to buyers.	Less effective sellers are deferential to customers, and are reluctant to have difficult and disagreeable conversations with buyers.
Understanding and navigating the sales cycle following the Stages to the Sale	Successful sellers have mastered the fundamentals of sales cycle navigation, including the Stages to the Sale. This seller often operates on autopilot when it comes to progressing through the sales cycle.	The least successful seller typically "flies by the seat of the pants" and lacks the discipline required to efficiently (maximum speed and least cost) and methodically move the deal process forward to close.

Sales-Force #2: The Ability to Build a Financial Business Case

My research revealed that the best sellers, those who win complex engagements and those who are successful at leading high-stakes projects, are the sellers who can sell financially. Fundamentally, every for-profit business wants the same few things: to grow profits, retain its top people, attract new customers, improve processes, and to engage with and retain customer; the most important being to increase profits—a metric that most public-company executives are measured on. So, not being able to financially justify a deal puts the seller at a disadvantage against competitors who can, and will likely, render the seller unable to demonstrate how his proposition directly contributes to the purpose or the achievement of the objective of the initiative for which their offering is being considered. At a minimum, the best sellers have the ability to:

- *Articulate the purpose of the project* under consideration, including the buyers' financial business objectives to be contributed to or achieved by engaging in the initiative.

- *Develop a cost-benefit justification* for their proposal including the project's Return on Investment (at a minimum), the project's Net Present Value (today's value of a net future financial benefit), the project's time to break-even or payback the initial investment, and, in some cases, work with the buyer to determine the project's Internal Rate of Return.

- *Tie the financial benefits of their proposal to the purpose* of the buyer's project in order to financially-justify the required investment in the proposal.

Financial Justification / Selling		
Characteristic	The Most Successful Sellers	The Least Successful Sellers
Articulate the buyer's financial business objectives and the purpose of the project	The successful sellers are adept at extracting the buyers' financial business objectives, validating the objectives, developing an offering that supports the achievement of the financial objectives, and tying the objectives to an initiative driven by the seller's proposal.	The least successful sellers have not developed the skills to articulate a buyer's requirements as financial business objectives.
Develop a cost-benefit justification for their proposal	The most productive sellers are skilled at developing the Cost-Benefit Analysis of their proposals, specifically, the Return on Investment and break-even period.	The least successful sellers do not understand how to develop a meaningful financial justification for their proposals (beyond Total Cost of Ownership), nor do they develop it.

Tie the financial benefits of their proposal to the purpose and financial objectives of the buyer's project	The successful sellers financially-justify their proposals by tying the financial benefits of their proposals to the financial objectives of the buyers' projects, thereby helping buyers justify making the required investment in the proposal.	The least successful sellers routinely fail to help the buyer understand why an investment in their proposal is a good financial decision. As a result, they are ineffective at justifying buyers' investments in their proposition.

Sales-Force #3: The Ability to Articulate the Value They and Their Company Bring

The top-tier sellers have the ability to articulate the value they bring to buyers by providing compelling answers to the buyer's question "Why do I Need You?" Given the technological advances over the past twenty years, buyers now have access to the same information as most sellers. While this does not constitute what game theorists would call *Perfect Information*—the assumption that if all buyers know all things, about all products, at all times, they will choose the best products and the market will reward those who make the best products with higher sales—it does mean that buyers are more informed in their decision-making and they have little-to-no use for sellers that provide no additional value. Plus, in many cases, buyers now have the ability to place orders electronically, rendering valueless-sellers nearly useless.

Not long ago, I was engaged by a top global, Germany-based pharmaceutical manufacturer to support a major initiative in which they were engaged. The company explained to me the things they had done in support of the project and the data they produced. I reviewed the information and instantly identified no fewer than ten things the team had done that would expose the company to high-stakes risks. The company's management team was not angry with me because I, in essence, told them they had wasted a lot of time and money. Instead, they said, "That's why we brought you in, to make sure that we weren't making a big mistake." To the pharmaceutical company, my value was helping them forestall what would have otherwise been certain risk exposures, saving the company lots of money and saving the managers their jobs.

The most effective sellers are always prepared to answer what I call *The Five Killer Questions* that buyers sometime ask. If a seller cannot answer these value-based questions from a prospective buyer, the seller not only runs the risk of appearing un-credible, they also risk being perceived as bringing no value to the buyer or the buyer's company. The Five Killer Questions are:

1. Who are you and why should I care?
2. What do you know about me or my company that

I couldn't simply find on Google?

3. "So What [regarding the seller's proposition]?" Why are you bothering me?

4. What makes you any different than the other 50 companies saying the same thing?

5. Why do you believe what you're telling me?

I call these The Five Killer Questions (5KQs) because every time I and my colleagues have witnessed buyers asking these questions to a seller and the seller was unable to satisfactorily answer any of these questions (to the prospective buyer's liking), the buyers immediately began to write-off the seller as another "me-too" peddler who brought nothing beneficial to the buyer's business.

Using the table below, describe how you would answer the value-related questions presented in the table to see if yours are closer to the characteristics of the most successful sellers (who can fluidly answer each of these value-based questions) or the least successful sellers (who cannot answer the questions, leading the prospective buyer to question the value they bring, their usefulness, and even their credibility).

"Why do I Need *YOU*?"	
Customer Challenge	**Your Response**
I can simply go to the Internet and find out everything about your products, services, and solutions that I need to know (including prices) and more information than you can provide me with. So why do I need you?	
I can place an order through the Internet, and in fact, I can find multiple sources for your same products / offerings, too. So why do I need you?	
When I have a problem, I can simply call your Customer Service department and they can address my concern just as effectively (and probably faster) than you can, can't they? So why do I need you?	
I've been in this business for 25 years. I probably know more about *your* products, services, and solutions than *you* do. What can you possibly tell me that I don't already know?	
What can you do for me that I can't simply do on my own?	

Sales-Force #4: Establish Credibility

Of all the characteristics of the most successful sales professionals that my team and I have studied, the most important attribute of the most productive sellers is credibility. To the buyer, a credible seller is believable and trustworthy. This is important because the data show that buyers often accept and execute the credible sellers' recommendations based heavily on the fact that the buyer trusts that the credible seller will not steer him wrong, believes that the credible seller has the buyers' best interest at heart, and—like E.F. Hutton—when the credible seller talks, buyers listen.

Credible sellers have strong *business acumen*. They understand business strategy and how business works—especially the buyer's business and the industry in which the buyer competes—and they demonstrate this knowledge as it relates to the buyer's business and any related initiative being considered to support the buyer's business goals and objectives. This business acumen enables the successful seller to sell *consultatively*, by not asking "What can I sell to this buyer?" but instead, asking "What business objectives is this buyer trying to accomplish and how can I help them accomplish them?" By focusing on the buyer's business goals, objectives, and general business strategy, the consultative seller often positions him/herself as (and becomes) part of the buyer's project team since the buyer sees the consultative seller not as some pushy salesperson who's only interest is getting the buyer to purchase their products, but as a resource whose interest is in helping the buyer resolve the *buyer's* business issues.

BUSINESS ACUMEN
The Credible Seller

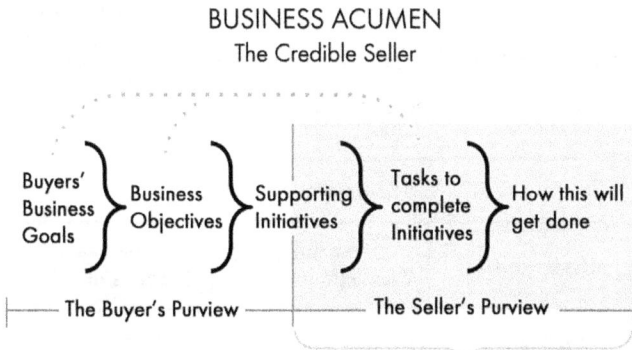

| Buyers' Business Goals | } | Business Objectives | } | Supporting Initiatives | } | Tasks to complete Initiatives | } | How this will get done |

|————— The Buyer's Purview —————|————— The Seller's Purview —————|

The credible (and most successful) seller owns this level of the business discussion and can effectively tie it back to the Customer's Purview, establishing herself as a leader in the eyes of the buyer.

The most successful sellers also contribute to the buyer's perception of their credibility by demonstrating—on the fly—their ability to use the buyer's business objectives articulated during the discussion as the starting point for defining ways they can help the buyer achieve the business objectives. These sellers' ideas are not canned or presented on company datasheets, but are, instead, developed on the fly, often using a napkin, pen & paper, a whiteboard, or a digital device (e.g. a computer tablet using a writing instrument as a pen) to work through compelling scenarios toward the resolution of a problem or the achievement of an objective. By doing this, the successful sellers take the lead in the discussion (and ultimately, the initiative) and demonstrate themselves to be a valuable resource the prospective buyer should be comfortable following.

Credibility		
Characteristic	**The Most Successful Sellers**	**The Least Successful Sellers**
Business acumen	The successful sellers are knowledgeable about business strategy and how business works. And they are especially knowledgeable about how the *buyer's* business works and how it is positioned within the industry in which the buyer competes.	The least successful sellers have a marginal understanding of how business works and often are ignorant about business strategy and its importance to the performance of a company.

The ability to conceptually define solutions to problems and ideas for accomplishing business objectives on the fly	The most productive sellers have the experience and confidence to talk about business problems and solution concepts at any moment with a prospective buyer. And they do this without the benefit of prepared notes, using a piece of paper or a whiteboard to lead the discussion.	The least successful sellers do not have the confidence or experience to act "off the cuff" and lead a discussion about problem resolution without the support of prepared notes and talking points.
Skilled at taking the lead of buyers' initiatives related to solutions the seller can provide in support of the initiatives	The successful sellers realize the importance of taking the leadership position with buyer initiatives (especially when competition is involved) and they earn the right to do so through their demonstrated business savvy and their earned credibility.	Ineffective sellers rarely command the leadership of customer initiatives.
Selling consultatively	The most successful and respected sellers (by their customers and peers) approach sales opportunities from a consultative approach, rightly giving buyers the impression that the seller's interest is in helping the buyer as part of the buyer's team, *not* as simply a salesperson.	The least effective sellers struggle to sell consultatively because they lack an understanding of basic business strategy and they struggle with the notion that they should "stop belligerently selling and start supporting."

Sales-Force #5: The Ability to Mollify Buyers' Constrictive Buying-Emotions of Fear and Skepticism

Buying Emotions play a major role in a seller's ability to even begin to engage with a prospective buyer or even a suspect about making a purchase. If, for instance, a buyer is fearful or skeptical about engaging with a seller about the prospect of making a purchase decision, the seller will not be successful in the sales cycle until that buyer has been moved from those constrictive Buying Emotions of *fear* and *skepticism* to a state of calm and openness to consideration. That is why a seller's ability to allay a buyer's fears and skepticism is critical, and doing so most often begins with gaining the buyer's trust and *piquing the buyer's interest* about the benefits (value) of engaging with the seller— just enough—so that the buyer is curious about where such an engagement can lead and wants to learn more about it. This is where a seller's ability to pique a prospective buyer's interest up-front is valuable.

Piquing a buyer's interest is about accomplishing two things: (1) making the buyer curious about the seller's intriguing statements, and (2) making the buyer want to hear more about the proposition contained in the seller's statements. We have found, and it has been our experience, that the most effective sellers welcome the buyer's questions (and even objections) that follow the seller's *piquing interest* statements. The reason is because it is a sign that the prospective buyer is open to consideration, the buyer is trying to address a problem that the seller's statements suggest can help, and that the buyer will want to move the discussion to the next stage of the sales cycle.

The idea behind piquing interest is nothing new; some refer to the activity as giving an "elevator pitch" and some refer to it as delivering an "Initial Benefit Statement" (IBS). Whatever it is called, the central idea is consistent: state your case as to why the prospective buyer should want to continue a discussion with you about helping the buyer resolve some issue or achieve some business objective ... and do it in less than one minute! The seller's piquing interest statement should answer the buyer's unspoken question: "Why should I care to spend my valuable time talking with you?" Oftentimes, the crafting of the piquing interest statement requires the seller to be creative, imaginative, and present something that is unanticipated in order to break through the clutter of the other 50 sellers who contact the prospective buyer every week.

Mollify Buyers' Constrictive Buying Emotions

Characteristic	The Most Successful Sellers	The Least Successful Sellers
Move the prospective buyer from the Buying Emotions of fear and skepticism	The successful sellers are able to establish credibility with prospective buyers. This—along with the sellers' ability to compel the buyer to want to hear more about the sellers' proposition by effectively answering the question "Why should I care to spend my valuable time talking with you?"—encourages the buyers to lower their guard and move beyond their Buying Emotions of *fear* and *skepticism*.	The least successful sellers struggle to move fearful and skeptical buyers from these initial Buying Emotions because they lack credibility with the prospective buyers and they are unaccustomed to crafting and delivering piquing interest statements.
Craft and deliver a compelling piquing interest statement	The successful sellers are experienced (having more than 7 years of selling experience), and their varied experiences and frequent customer engagements help them to craft compelling piquing interest statements that move the prospective buyer to the next desired stage of the sales cycle.	The least successful sellers rarely craft piquing interest statements, and when they do, the statements are not compelling and are ineffective at moving the prospective buyer to the subsequent stage of the sales cycle.

Models of Selling

The previous discussion about The Five Forces of Movement begs the question: If the most successful sellers master and execute these forces in the normal course of doing their jobs, and that execution makes them far more productive, effective, and successful than sellers who do not, then what does that mean about the various models of selling which also claim to breed the best sellers?

The answer is this: In my more than 25 years of sales experience and studying the profession of selling, I have come to learn that most, if not all, of the various models of selling introduced over the last 65 years are all based on a few variously-worded, fundamental concepts: being consultative in one's approach; establishing credibility; understanding business (business acumen); articulating and demonstrating value; and selling to business objectives (often requiring financial selling). Whether it's ...

- Consultative selling
- Direct selling
- Strategic Selling
- Guaranteed Sale selling
- Needs-based selling
- Persuasive selling

- SPIN Selling
- Hard Selling
- Heart Selling
- Price-based selling
- Relationship Selling
- Target account selling
- Solution selling
- Sandler selling
- 5-P selling
- Challenger selling
- Action Selling
- or SNaP selling (a model I developed)

… they are all fundamentally based on the few core concepts I described above. I liken it to an automobile: one manufacturer takes a drive train, a chassis, an electrical system, an exterior body, and seats & an interior, and call it a Honda Accord. Another manufacturer takes the same core elements—and adds a few inconsequential things—and calls it a Toyota Corolla. Regardless of what they call the respective cars, the cars are ALL built on the same five core elements—a drive train, a chassis, an electrical system, an exterior body, and seats & an interior—and they are all designed to serve one primary function: transport people from point A to point B. And let's face it: none of the models of selling that have been introduced in the last decade are a *Tesla*.

So, whether it's the "Challenger" model or the "SPIN" model or even my "SNaP" model, there is nothing new; the same core concepts have existed for tens of years, and—when it comes to effective selling—the most successful sellers integrate these concepts into their selling motions, reinterpreted as The Five Forces of Movement.

04

The Path Forward

The nature of selling has changed in the last handful of years: Buyers have access to technology and heretofore-unavailable information, making them as knowledgeable, as independent, and as savvy as ever; the commoditization of certain once-distinguishable products, such as computer systems and brand-name pharmaceuticals, has relegated many sellers to the status of customer service reps and order-takers; sales companies no longer heavily invest in the training and development of its sales representatives; in an effort to reduce costs (specifically the cost of real estate), companies have shuttered spacious sales offices and have opted for the *hoteling* office model in which no seller has an assigned desk (after all, they should be out visiting prospects and customers). This model has led to a reduction in the number of opportunities a younger sales rep can get coaching and learn from the more seasoned sales reps; a seller's tenure working for the same company (including voluntary and involuntary attrition) is dramatically shorter than in ever has been. Companies do not seem to value sales reps as has been the case for the last 100 years. Today, many companies consider sales reps to be swappable with no noticeable degradation; and, lastly sales representatives simply do not sell as effectively as they have in years past.

My first *real* professional sales job was as a sales representative for the IBM Corporation. Sure, I had sold encyclopedias door-to-door, I worked as a phone salesperson, and I even sold inexpensive household items door-to-door as a precocious 13-year-old. But my job at IBM was the first significant sales job I ever held. In those days, upon joining IBM as a sales representative trainee, you spent the first 12 to 18 months in sales training and being coached-up by your office's seasoned sales professionals—and they were *good!* Word had it that IBM spent in the neighborhood of $100,000 per-person training its sales new-hires. Today, companies do not invest that heavily to train new-hires or anyone else on how to sell—not even IBM. Besides the sizeable investment IBM made in its sales reps' development, the amount of time we young sellers would spend with senior, highly-successful sales reps "learning the ropes" was almost as valuable as that $100,000 training investment. Sadly, those days are mostly gone, and the things companies did in the past to bolster their sales organizations are an anachronism today. If companies are to succeed given the changed climate for selling, they and their sellers will have to determine the best path forward based on what they determine to be the direction in which they want to go.

When I am engaged by sales companies looking to improve the overall performance and efficiency (as measured primarily by their cost-per-order-dollar) of their sales organizations, I am inevitably asked "What can we do moving forward that will help our sales operation and team of sellers maintain and/or achieve the highest level of performance?" My answers vary slightly depending on the nuances of the company's sales organization (e.g. the products they sell, the industry in which they compete, the experience level of their sales force, the nature of their sales, the size of the organization, their level of sales advancement, etc.) but I mostly provide any combination of the following best practices:

Develop a Strategy

Companies develop strategies for two fundamental purposes: (1) to determine how the company will create value; and (2) to gain a competitive advantage. Though many managers think otherwise, every business, company, and organization that wants to accomplish "something important" needs a strategy to do so most efficiently. A strategy is simply a plan that defines how a company will accomplish the things (*goals*) it has determined are important to its competitiveness, performance, and viability. Any company that engages in activities that are not guided by a well-reasoned strategy is not only guaranteed to be wasting time on irrelevant activities, but also operating at suboptimal levels. And for companies that have developed strategies, any activities the company's associates engage in that are not in support of the company's strategy and goals are wasted efforts, too.

For many sales organizations, the idea of developing a strategy seems like a long, academic, unnecessary exercise in futility. And it's understandable: many managers have no experience with developing and executing strategies, so to them, the idea is not only intimidating, but also, in their opinion, "We've done well without one for all these years so why start now?" That's unfortunate because **business initiatives that are pursued under the direction of a well-reasoned strategy are 60% more successful** than those which are not. First, let me state that the concept of a strategy is rather simple: you define the reason why your company is in business and, based on that, you determine the things the company must do to stay in business, and then you develop an action plan to do those things. To prove my point about the simplicity of the strategy concept, I will provide you with a basic understanding of strategy using only 4 easy-to-understand bullet points:

1. A strategy is a plan that defines what a company must do to prosper (*goals*) and how the company will accomplish those things (*action plan*). A *Goal* is a broad intended outcome of an initiative or an activity in which the company is engaged, and it takes the form of "To [Action Verb] [Noun]." For example, a simple-yet-common sales goal could be "To [Grow] the [Customer Base]."

2. An *Objective* is the measurable (usually quantitative) manifestation of the *Goal* which it supports. In other words, the Objective defines in measurable/quantitative (and time-specific) terms how the company will know that it has accomplished the Goal which the Objective supports. For example, if

the Goal is "To Grow the Customer Base," and last year the company serviced 200 customers, then the Objective would be defined in such a way that—if it is achieved—the company knows it would have accomplished their Goal. Such an Objective could be defined as: "Achieve a customer base of 201 customers by December 31st," or "Gain 20 new customers by December 31st in order to bring our customer count to 201."

3. Once the Goal(s) and Objective(s) have been defined, specific *Initiatives* must be defined in support of an Objective. An *Initiative* is a project or other undertaking that defines what must be done in order to achieve the Objective it supports. So, if the Objective is to "Achieve a customer base of 201 customers by December 31st," the associated Initiative must define the project or undertaking that will lead to at least 201 customers by December 31st.

4. Once the Initiatives are defined, an *Action Plan* (or "Task List") must be developed which defines the specific tasks/actions that must be executed in order to complete the Initiative it supports. The *Action Plan* defines the tasks/action items, resources needed to complete them, person(s) responsible

for their completion, and the expected completion date for each.

THE STRATEGY CONCEPT

This, ladies & gentlemen, is fundamentally what a strategy is all about; it is a road map that defines specifically how you will accomplish the goals you establish for your business. And by effectively *executing* the strategy (a critical requirement), the sales group will likely improve its competitive position in the market and deliver stakeholder value.

Develop a Sales Playbook

I believe that a strategy and a Sales Playbook go hand-in-hand: the strategy defines what must be done and how it will be done, while the Playbook translates the strategy down to the field-level, giving the sales team the best opportunity to execute their portion of the strategy. The Playbook is about strategy *execution*—the primary reason why most strategies fail.

Another benefit of the Sales Playbook is that it not only focuses the sales team's efforts on the things they must do to help the company excel, it also brings alignment to the organization by ensuring that the activities in which the sales team is engaged (dictated by the Playbook which is driven by the strategy) are in alignment with the activities the company's executive team have defined as important. The Playbook can be seen as part of a behavioral plan that drives the behaviors in the sales team that the company's management team covets.

While the contents of a Sales Playbook vary company-to-company, the most common segments include some form of the following:

- Organization Overview
- 12 to 24-month Sales Goals to be achieved (including revenue goals)
- [Quarterly] Sales Initiatives to be executed
- Territory and Account Management guidance
- The Company's Sales Process (and the initiatives to be executed at each stage of the process)
- Roles & Responsibilities

- Sales Guidance (e.g. Consultative Selling guidelines, Strategic Selling guidelines, etc.)
- Sales Tool Support (e.g. Sales Navigator +lus documentation, planning forms, CRM Quick Reference Cards, coaching forms & guides, etc.)
- The Expected Sales Competencies (i.e. the minimal expectations of the sales team)

Develop and Actively Manage a Territory Plan

Time Management and *Territory Management* are best defined as "getting the most out of your sales day by planning the most efficient use of scarce resources." Territory planning incorporates Time and Territory Management and is about efficiency—conducting business in the most expedient manner with the fewest wasted motions at the lowest cost. Done correctly, a Territory Plan helps the seller with Time Management by helping the seller balance time for prospecting, time for sales calls, time for demonstrations, time for tours, time for closing, and, necessarily, time for administrative tasks and paperwork. It also influences Territory Management through its requirements for achieving the sales territory's objectives, mapping & routing, customer touches, and prioritization. One risky assumption I am making is that, prior to a sales organization implementing a Territory Planning routine, the organization has effectively *aligned* the territory, addressing imbalance in sales territory assignments by balancing territory coverage per sales rep and matching coverage requirements with customer needs. Territory Plans commonly consist of:

- Territory Objectives
- Account Plans
- Territory Management activities
- Communication Plans (Note: I have included a Territory Review outline in the Appendix of this book)

There is a relationship between Strategic Planning (the process of developing a strategy), Territory Management, and Account Planning, all elements of a Territory Plan. The sales strategy informs the Territory Plan—what sellers and managers will do to maximize their efforts and results within a given territory or assignment. A *territory* is merely a collection of prospects, accounts, and sales goal, and the plans the seller creates for each account (*Account Plans*) collectively form the seller's Territory Plan.

PLANNING RELATIONSHIPS

Start → **Strategic Plan**

Territory

Accounts
- Account 1
- Account 2
- Account 3
- Account 4
- Account 5

Account Plan

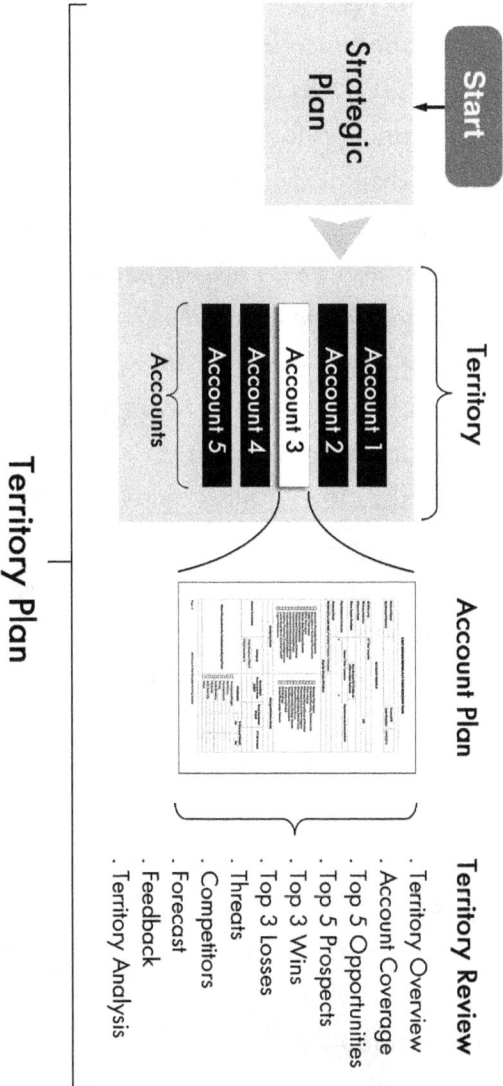

Territory Plan

Territory Review
. Territory Overview
. Account Coverage
. Top 5 Opportunities
. Top 5 Prospects
. Top 3 Wins
. Top 3 Losses
. Threats
. Competitors
. Forecast
. Feedback
. Territory Analysis

Develop a Sales Force Effectiveness Program

According to a Consumer Product executive survey from July/August 2011, "sales effectiveness" is ranked among the top 5 priorities for 90% of the respondents, however, less than half of them believe their salesforce is operating at maximum effectiveness levels. My definition of Sales Effectiveness is *proficiency at accomplishing a goal or producing the intended sales results; sales activities performed with a degree of skill or competence.* Like the Consumer Product survey, my experience has also shown that sales executives want their sellers to be highly-effective at their job. While executives may want their sellers to be "highly-effective," the challenge for the executives with whom I have worked over the years is that they rarely develop a sales effectiveness program designed to ensure that their sales professionals are, indeed, highly-effective.

A Sales Force Effectiveness Program is not simply a program to get every sales rep to complete a course on Solution Selling or some other model of selling. It is a *program* designed to improve the overall effectiveness of the sales team, which implies that sales organizations must first define what *they* consider to be *effective* and then build a complete program designed to take the sales team (including managers) from their current state of "mostly ineffective" to the desired state of "effective."

Sales effectiveness programs are not overnight fixes, they are programs designed to understand a company's sales inventory and, over time, improve the seller's performance from where it is today to where the company wants it to be.

The development of a Sales Force Effectiveness Program should begin with company managers asking three fundamental questions related to the creation of the program:

1. What are we trying to accomplish?
2. How will we know that a change is an improvement?
3. What changes can we make that will result in improvement?

At a minimum, any Sales Effectiveness Program should include the following elements:

- Define what you consider to be "effective" and establish the minimum sales standards to being considered effective. I recommend starting by define indicators of sales "effectiveness" (e.g. average revenue per account; average opportunity size; average order margin; average time to proposal; administrative time spent vs. productive selling time, etc.).

- Benchmark the sales team's current performance levels against the effectiveness standard you establish (preferably through testing).

- Develop a *Gap Analysis*: Using the benchmark data, evaluate the sales team members' major deficiencies and identify the improvement needed to reach the minimum or desired standard of effectiveness.

- Develop a training curriculum designed to upgrade the sales skills of sellers and managers (including coaching skills), improve on the areas of deficiency, and close the effectiveness gap.

- Define Key Performance Indicators (KPIs), measurement criteria, and processes by which to gauge the effectiveness of the sales training effort and the sellers' progress.

- Make available the tools and reporting necessary for the sales team to meet the effectiveness standards.

- Test at the midpoint and test at the end of the predefined program testing period. Determine consequences or next-steps for reps who do not meet the qualification criteria.

- Measure the company, business unit, region, territory, and seller' performance levels pre-and post-effectiveness program implementation to gauge the program's and the sales team's overall performance improvement and the success or failure of the initiative.

Get Back to Basics

Over the years, I have trained, coached, developed, managed, and mentored tens of thousands of sellers across different countries, and the one thing that sticks out about sellers more than anything else is the lack of those who have mastered the fundamentals of selling. What's equally surprising to me is that most companies ignore that fact. When companies today provide sales training to the sales organizations, it is one-size-fits-all, regardless of how disparate the relative sales skills are between the organization's sales reps; rookie new-hires are sent to the same training class as sellers with 20 years of experience based on an erroneous assumption that they all know how to fundamentally sell. In my experience, that is wishful thinking. If you manage sales reps, are skeptical about my assertion, and believe that all of your reps have mastered the fundamentals of selling, then here's a challenge: randomly select one of your "best" sales reps and ask him or her to "Describe the objection handling process," or "How do you calculate the ROI of a project?" or "How do you qualify a customer?" The latter is sort of a trick question because you can qualify an *opportunity* the customer is managing (are the funds available to pay for this? Has C-level management approved the project?), or you can qualify the customer herself (if it delivers the value you demand, will you buy it?). The point is that—in my estimation—75% of professional sellers are not proficient at executing sales fundamentals. And despite this, companies invest many thousands of dollars training these fundamentally-deficient sellers on the sales-model-of-the-day which often requires the sales fundamentals to be ingrained if the sales-model-of-the-day is to be effective.

I recommend that before a company spends any money on sales training moving forward, they first gauge the need for their sales teams to improve on the basics or to become well-versed in the sales fundamentals. I believe that after sellers have mastered the selling basics, they will not only improve their performance noticeably, but they will also have established the foundation necessary for other models of selling to be more meaningful and impactful.

Implement a "Type" Sales Compensation Plan

Let's face it: Many sales reps are stealing money from their companies. The sellers are being paid to *sell* stuff, but the majority of the time they are simply taking orders—something that can be more efficiently handled by a website. As sellers, we have all benefitted from the occasional "bluebird" (an unexpected, unplanned sales deal that comes from out of nowhere), and I, just like everyone else, have taken my share of orders. But I have never come across a company that uses the compensation plan to reward the people who actually *sell* a deal more significantly than they reward the people who simply take orders. For example, sellers who have to go through the rigors of moving a buyer to a sales win would earn a 3% commission on the deal, whereas sellers who simply take an order would earn a 0.5% commission on the deal. Naturally, implementing such a compensation model would require the company to establish clear criteria for defining a sale versus an order taken; define a process for identifying up front (in the funnel?) which opportunities are likely to be sales versus orders taken; and a process for tracking opportunities throughout the sales cycle in case there is a need to change a sale to an order taken, or vice versa (in many sales organizations, this type of funnel management cadence is practiced today). But in the end, it is doable.

The benefits of implementing such a Type Sales Compensation Plan include:

- Motivate the reps to engage in more valuable deals (those which are typically competitive, larger in scope & dollar volume, require the seller to sell, and have a longer sales cycle).

- Reward sellers for actual *sales* performance (what they are primarily hired to do) as opposed to rewarding them for doing nothing more than a website does.

- Improved sales skills by engaging in more deals that require the sellers to *sell*.

- Save the company money or, at worst, not cost the company any more than it does today in variable sales compensation. The reason is because, when you increase one commission rate (the rate for a real *sale*) and lower the other (the rate for taking an order), the average commissions payable will balance out. And if the average commissions payable increase, that's a good thing because it means the company is gaining more business.

Use Data and Analytics to Refine Targeting

Studies show that companies can increase sales revenue by approximately 400% through effective targeting versus a random approach for identifying and pursuing opportunities.

Today, there are so many CRM and sales analytics tools on the market that provide usable data that could help companies more effectively target growth opportunities and sellers more effectively target prospects, that it is surprising that only a small percentage of companies use the available data for effective targeting. While most companies use some form of sales tool, a smaller percentage of them extract all of the available date (or purchase add-on modules that will allow for such compilation and extraction), rendering the sales tools semi-useful.

Implement a Deal Loss Review Program

I have a saying that "The most valuable thing a sales professional can gain from winning a deal is the same thing they gain from losing one: experience. For varied experiences help you win more deals and lose fewer, enriching you both personally and professionally."

Although no seller ever wants to lose a deal, it is inevitable. But losing a deal is not a total loss. There is lots of valuable information that companies can learn from deal losses, information that can help the company improve its deficiencies (especially those that contributed to the loss) to become more competitive and win a higher percentage of deals moving forward. When a seller wins a deal, everyone is happy and the sales manager blasts email messages across the company describing how truly "great" the sales team was in winning the deal, how much of a "team effort" it was, and how the team simply ripped the competition to shreds. But when a seller *loses* a deal, there's total silence. No email blasts. No parties. No pats on the back. We never hear how "poorly-prepared" the sales team was or how uncoordinated the "team effort." We never hear about how the competition "ripped us to shreds." Instead, all we hear is some flavor of "They beat us on price."

Several years ago I was engaged by a top-3 global technology company to evaluate its sales team. As part of the effort, I compiled nearly 110 post-deal review write-ups explaining why a deal was won and why a deal was lost; although inconsistent, this company did conduct post-deal reviews. In total, there were approximately 90 win reviews and 20 loss reviews (hmmm). In 100% of the win reviews, the primary reason given for the win was the sales team's greatness. However, there was only ONE deal-loss review that listed the reason for the loss as the sales rep's ineffectiveness; one! This, of course, was nonsense. Is it possible that every *win* was due to the sales team's efforts and only one *loss* was due to the sales team's efforts? Possible, but unlikely. Deal-loss reviews are useless if the real reason for the loss is not captured, because it does not tell the management team what needs to be fixed in order to make the company more competitive or its offerings more viable.

Deal-loss reviews—as well as win reviews—reveal deficiencies and opportunities related to a company's sales strategies, its competitors' strategies, seller effectiveness, and the strength of the company's offerings. These things have an impact on a company's competitiveness, growth, and profitability. The insight that can be gleaned from a deal-loss review is so valuable that companies hire outside agencies to conduct the reviews on their behalf, especially when customer feedback is of interest.

We believe that deal-loss reviews should be conducted in multiple parts: one review with the direct sales team; one review with the sales manager(s) of the losing team members; one review with any sales extensions (partner companies, other divisions, 3rd parties with whom the company partnered in pursuit of the deal, etc.); and one review with the prospect or customer, going straight to the source to get their feedback on why the company was not awarded the deal. As you can imagine, the sales team's version of why the deal was lost and the prospect's or customer's version can differ dramatically. But in the end, the customer's facts trump the sales team's opinions. The good news, however, is that when sellers know that the company will be conducting deal-loss reviews and soliciting feedback from the prospect/customer, it motivates the sales team to be more forthright about what really took place during the sales engagement.

I recommend incorporating the following elements into a deal-loss review:

- Establish the deal background: the parties involved in the sales engagement, the length of the sales cycle, the customers involved in the decision process, the competitors involved.

- Understand the reason for the loss. Interview the sales team, the sales extensions involved in the deal, and the prospect or customer. Learn of the sales team's activities at each stage of the sales cycle (did they do everything "right"?). Note the winning competitive solution/proposal, the impact of the loss, and the cost-per-order-dollar (CPOD).

- Synthesize the information and develop a plan (strategy) that addresses the shortcomings (if any) that were identified as contributing to the loss.
- Execute the plan and follow up periodically on its progress.

Reduce and Eliminate Sales Detractors

As I wrote previously, sales detractors are activities that sellers engage in which do not advance the sales process. The more time spent on sales detractors, the less time (available to be) spent on selling activities that lead to a closed deal, and, consequently, the less revenue generated from customers and the lower the customer-retention rate. A list of common sales detractors includes:

- Managing e-mail
- Reporting & paperwork
- Using sales tools
- Conference calls / sales meetings
- Handling A/R and credit issues
- Duplication of effort
- Completing duplicate requests
- Technical issues
- Travel ("windshield time")
- Customer service-related activities
- "Useless" training
- Handling pricing and contract issues

Implement a Formal Sales Training Routine

All sales professionals should receive some form of formal sales training annually. However, sales reps do not significantly improve their sales performance if the lessons learned in the training are not exercised regularly and the practices do not become part of the sellers' natural selling motion or repertoire. In order to maximize the effectiveness of a sales training class, companies must provide periodic (quarterly?) reinforcing development activities that force the seller to execute the desired practices regularly so that the practices become unintimidating and second nature to the seller. A basic Sales Training Routine could look like this:

1. One annual sales training class.

2. Six monthly sales simulations and role play scenarios that reinforce the desired lessons taught in the training class.

3. Quarterly sales case studies in which the sales coach or manager presents the seller with a sales scenario related to a particular sales concept as taught in the sales training session.

These sales reinforcements, in addition to the sales training class, will have a noticeable impact on the sellers' adoption of the desired sales development behaviors which should improve the sellers' overall performance. The same routine could be applied to sales managers as a way of helping them to become better sales coaches. In this case, the sales simulations and sales case studies will be supplemented with a (quarterly) coaching effectiveness routine.

05

Art of Movement Workshop
for Sales Development. Manager-led

This chapter of the book includes a template for the development of an Art of Movement Workshop. The template can be used by sales managers and sellers alike to develop a program intended to help sellers better execute Buyer Movement. It does this by ensuring improvement in the sellers' overall sales effectiveness through mastery of The Five Sales-Forces.

The Art of Movement refers to sellers' ability to motivate Buyer Movement through the 4 stages based on Buying Emotions:

- Stage 1: Fear to Skepticism
- Stage 2: Skepticism to Calm & Openness
- Stage 3: Calm & Openness to Interest
- Stage 4: Interest to Action Mode

THE 4 STAGES of BUYER MOVEMENT
And the Relative Magnitude of their Barrier to Gaining a Sale

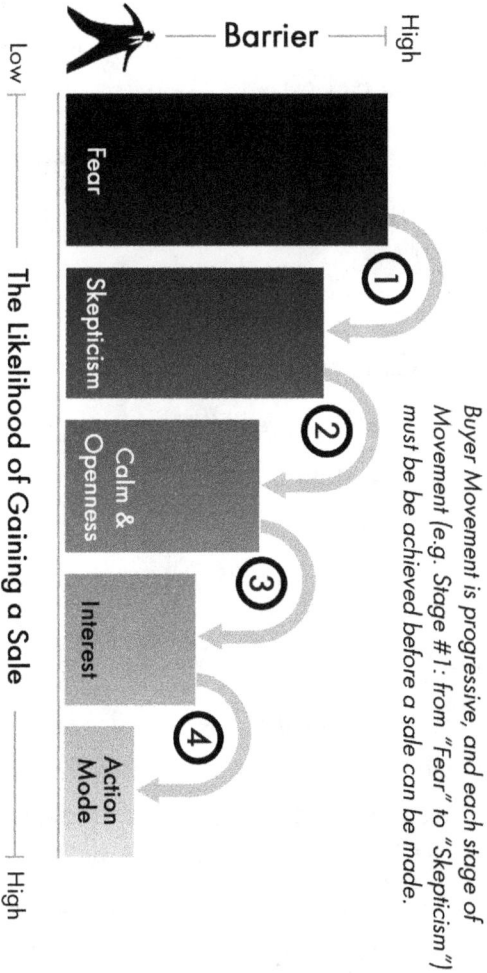

Barrier	High — Low

Fear

Skepticism

Calm & Openness

Interest

Action Mode

The Likelihood of Gaining a Sale

Low ——— High

Buyer Movement is progressive, and each stage of Movement (e.g. Stage #1: from "Fear" to "Skepticism") must be be achieved before a sale can be made.

Movement requires force, and Buyer Movement requires *Sale-Force*. The workshop reinforces the Art of Movement by providing a guide map based on the characteristics of the most successful sellers, characteristics that define The Five Sales-Forces.

- *Sales-Force #1*: Mastery of the Sales Fundamentals

- *Sales-Force #2*: The Ability to Build a Financial Business Case

- *Sales-Force #3*: The Ability to Articulate the Value they and their Company Bring

- *Sales-Force #4*: Establish Credibility

- *Sales-Force #5*: The Ability to Mollify Buyers' Constrictive Buying-Emotions of Fear and Skepticism

How the Workshop Works

Using the templates provided below, the sales manager will evaluate each of his or her sellers against the characteristics of each of the Five Sales-Forces. For example, for *Sales-Force #1: Mastery of the Sales Fundamentals*, the sales manager will compare her impression of Bobby's sales characteristics against those contained in the Mastery of Sales Fundamentals template. The exercise will look something like this:

Mastery of Sales Fundamentals	
Characteristic	**Bobby's Acumen**
Listening and questioning for understanding	Good
Objection Handling	**Needs Improvement ◄**
Qualifying and closing; asking for the business	**Needs Improvement ◄**
Being forthright, open, & honest	Good
Understanding and navigating the sales cycle following the Stages to the Sale	Satisfactory

Based on this assessment, the manager will develop a plan to improve Bobby's effectiveness at objection handling and qualifying and closing, and will track progress periodically with Bobby as part of his development and performance plan. The manager will complete this process for each characteristic of each Sales-Force.

Templates

Sales-Force #1: Mastery of the Sales Fundamentals

Mastery of Sales Fundamentals	
Characteristic	**Seller's Acumen**
Listening and questioning for understanding	
Objection Handling	
Qualifying and closing; asking for the business	
Being forthright, open, & honest	
Understanding and navigating the sales cycle following the Stages to the Sale	

Sales-Force #2: The Ability to Build a Financial Business Case

Financial Justification / Selling	
Characteristic	**Seller's Acumen**
Articulate the buyer's financial business objectives and the purpose of the project	
Develop a cost-benefit justification for their proposal	
Tie the financial benefits of their proposal to the purpose and financial objectives of the buyer's project	

Sales-Force #3: The Ability to Articulate the Value they and their Company Bring

"Why Do I Need *YOU*?"	
Characteristic	**Seller's Acumen**
I can simply go to the Internet and find out everything about your products, services, and solutions that I need to know (including prices) and more information than you can provide me with. So why do I need you?	
I can place an order through the Internet, and in fact, I can find multiple sources for your same products / offerings, too. So why do I need you?	
When I have a problem, I can simply call your Customer Service department and they can address my concern just as effectively (and probably faster) than you can, can't they? So why do I need you?	
I've been in this business for 25 years. I probably know more about *your* products, services, and solutions than *you* do. What can you possibly tell me that I don't already know?	
What can you do for me that I can't simply do on my own?	

Sales-Force #4: Establish Credibility

Credibility	
Characteristic	**Seller's Acumen**
Business acumen	
The ability to conceptually define solutions to problems and ideas for accomplishing business objectives on the fly	
Skilled at taking the lead of buyers' initiatives related to solutions the seller can provide in support of the initiatives	
Selling consultatively	

Sales-Force #5: The Ability to Mollify Buyers' Constrictive Buying-Emotions of Fear and Skepticism

Mollify Buyers' Constrictive Buying Emotions	
Characteristic	**Seller's Acumen**
Move the prospective buyer from the Buying Emotions of fear and skepticism	
Craft and deliver a compelling *piquing interest* statement	

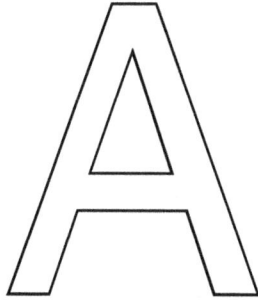

About the Author

Tab Edwards is a consultant, author, and lecturer with more than 25 years of experience in sales, strategy, consulting, and business management. He began his sales journey at the tender age of 13 selling inexpensive household items door-to-door. Since then, he has run a $2.6Billion sales organization and has held award-winning sales, management, and consulting positions at some of the world's most admired companies, including the IBM Corporation, General Electric, and Hewlett-Packard. Tab works with professionals around the world on becoming more effective sellers, and he works with companies to help them improve their overall sales performance. He is the author of seven books on the topics of sales, strategy, and business process improvement.

A

....

Appendix

....

Contents

....

Sample Sales Effectiveness Metrics

- Sales by product type
- Sales by geography
- New customers
- Sales to new vs. existing customers
- Forecast accuracy
- Expense management
- Average revenue per customer (up/down)
- Salesperson Ranking
- New account calls
- # of proposals submitted/ close ratio
- # of competitive wins/ losses
- Customer retention
- Lead-to-opportunity conversions
- Bid-to-win ratio
- Bid-to-close speed (Sales Cycle days)
- Average revenue per sale
- Market share change
- Profit per customer
- New customers
- Forecast accuracy
- Discounts offered
- Gross revenue
- Percentage of goal attainment
- Sales growth rate
- Gross profit
- % of reps above plan
- Account retention
- Sales-to-expense ratio
- Revenue per customer

- Lead conversion rate
- # of prospecting calls
- # of sales appointments
- Sales skills, aptitude, experience
- Assignment distribution
- Selling stages engaged
- Account management
- Coaching
- High-value activities
- Opportunity Management
- Account planning
- Customer service/sat
- Revenue/profit per customer
- Time management
- Business acumen
- Knowledge Management

Sample Territory Review Outline

1) Territory

    a) Describe the territory

    b) List of accounts in the territory

    c) Territory $ objective

2) Coverage

    a) How is your time prioritized?

    b) How will all (significant) accounts be touched regularly?

    c) How are account extensions (company)/3rd parties used?

3) Top 10 Opportunities (Existing Accounts)

    a) Account name

    b) Account size / Demographics

        i) Employees, locations, annual spend, etc.

    c) Opportunity description, including:

        i) Size ($ if it's quantitative)

        ii) Compelling event

        iii) Competitors engaged

        iv) Odds of winning

        v) Expected close date

    d) What is needed to win?

4) Top 10 Prospects

    a) Account name

    b) Account size/Demographics

        i) Employees, locations, annual spend, etc.

    c) Why is this a top-10 prospect?

    d) Competitor incumbent

    e) What is needed to win?

    f)   What is being done to develop new accounts in the territory?

5) **Major (Top 3) Wins**
    a)   Account name
    b)   What did we "win"?
        i)   If monetary, quantify
    c)   What was the reason for each win?
    d)   Learnings that can be shared?

6) **Major (Top 3) Losses**
    a)   Account name
    b)   What did we "lose"?
        i)   If monetary, quantify
    c)   Who was the successful competitor?
    d)   Why did they win?
    e)   What could have been done differently?
    f)   Learnings that can be shared?

7) **Threats**
    a)   What accounts are in danger of losing?
        i)   Why?
        ii)   What is being done to avert this?

8) **Competitors**
    a)   Who is prominent in the territory?
    b)   Where they win, why do they win?
    c)   Where they lose, why do they lose?
    d)   What can we do to compete more effectively with them?

9) **Your Feedback**
    a)   What can we do to support your personal success?
    b)   What can we do to help you win/close more business?

c) What should the company be doing that we are not?

d) What is missing from our portfolio?

e) Other?

10) Forecast

a) If forecasting a miss, why?

i) What is needed to change this forecast to a make?

Index

THE WATER TRAINING INSTITUTE
SINCE 1987